Memoirs · David Ben-Gurion

MEMOIRS

COMPILED BY THOMAS R. BRANSTEN

David Ben-Gurion

THE WORLD PUBLISHING COMPANY

NEW YORK AND CLEVELAND

First published in the United States of America
by The World Publishing Company
2231 West 110th Street, Cleveland, Ohio 44102

First printing 1970

Copyright © 1970 by
Covenant Communications Corporation, Geneva, Switzerland

Library of Congress Catalog Card Number: 72-123707

WORLD PUBLISHING
TIMES MIRROR

PRINTED IN GREAT BRITAIN

CONTENTS

PREFACE

'Words without deeds,' says David Ben-Gurion, 'are nothing.' And he adds: 'One must show the way by example.'

If anyone has set an example in the conduct of his life, Ben-Gurion is certainly that person. He has lived his thoughts in his day-to-day actions and he has devoted his entire existence to a single end: the redemption of the Jewish people in their ancient home of Israel.

Now that he can look back over sixty years in this country and to a life of Jewish activism that encompasses eight decades – four-fifths of a century! – the thoughts of Ben-Gurion must claim the attention of all who have shared in the Jewish experience. But though he takes the Jews as his subject in this book, he carries his wisdom to a plane of universality. Ben-Gurion likes to invoke the Prophet Isaiah who enjoined the Jews to be 'a light unto the nations'. Here, he himself has kept faith with this injunction. Any human being who has reflected on the meaning of his days and on human existence in general will find in this volume food for thought and for inspiration.

What strikes me about these meditations are their youthfulness, the flexibility of Ben-Gurion's approach to the problems he examines, the rigour of his logic and, not least, his sharp sense of humour. This is not an 'old man's' book hearking with nostalgia for things past. When Ben-Gurion recalls former days he does so to illuminate present and future.

The words set down here are those of a fighter who is also a logician, a wit and a philosopher. His long existence, far from dulling the edge of a sharp perception, has endowed it with a mellowness, a breadth of vision and a profundity that no one who has lived less fully or less wisely could hope to attain.

Ben-Gurion writes of Moses whom he calls by his Hebrew name of Moshe. He says that Moshe gave the Jews a definition of their mission, a reason for their presence as a people. And he adds that today, 3,300 years later, this definition is as meaningful as when first formulated. In other words, all things in life change yet certain ideas and principles by the truth they embody abide for all time.

I think that what Ben-Gurion offers us in this study also contains elements of enduring truth. It is not a difficult work to read or to understand. But it does reflect the sagacity of a life lived in dedication to an ideal by a man who is an activist in the strongest sense of the term and equally a thinker of penetration. I take great honour and pleasure in commending this volume both to a Jewish and a general public not only for the occasion of a single reading but as one of those enduring books to keep, to treasure, to study periodically throughout one's days, to hand on to one's children. And most of all, to learn from by a man whose life and whose words form a whole that is truly exemplary.

ABRAHAM F. RAD
Honorary Chairman
Israel Communications Center, Jerusalem

INTRODUCTION

HILD of the Polish ghetto, immigrant to Palestine, farm labourer and pioneer, political organizer, statesman, founder of the Israel Defence Forces and their first commander-in-chief, kibbutznik, scholar, David Ben-Gurion has in the course of eighty-odd years lived many lives.

Politically, he stands among the great of his time as a shaper of history. Like all larger-than-life leaders he has known adulation and hatred, has been followed and denied. But he has marked the twentieth century with his presence and, so doing, has changed the lives of many.

Principal mobilizer of the Jewish consciousness after the Second World War and architect of Israel's re-birth in nationhood, Ben-Gurion guided his country as its first Prime Minister through fifteen crucial years. More than any other individual, he bears responsibility for defending the young state against the onslaught of seven Arab armies, for shaping the machinery of government, establishing the educational system and bringing into existence many other institutions vital to national life. His efforts were instrumental in advancing agriculture, the extraordinary fertilization of an arid soil that is Israel's pride, and in maintaining the security of his people against their neighbours' perennial hostility.

Over and above his actions, Ben-Gurion has become through a lifetime of single-minded devotion to Israel's cause a symbol of the continuing struggle to provide the

Jewish people with a national home. In the Ben-Gurion philosophy, Israel did not spring magically to life in 1948 by act of the United Nations. This legalization merely confirmed the reality of a Jewish presence brought about by laborious struggle, a struggle that must go on. The House of Israel, according to Ben-Gurion, has been and must continue to be built where nothing stood before, by the toil of Jewish hands and brains, defended with Jewish blood, affirming a will to survive beyond repudiation and holocaust, a living example of the pioneer virtues for all mankind.

In daily life a modest man who opposes protocol with the informality of the farmer-pioneer, Ben-Gurion's words and deeds have always provoked thought, excitement, controversy no matter how softly spoken or unobtrusively executed. His retirement from government in June 1963 is a case in point. It has been described as spectacularly unspectacular. He simply announced his departure at a routine Cabinet meeting and left next day for a Negev kibbutz in that same desert wilderness of Zin where Moses wandered with the children of Israel four thousand years ago. There, as a member of the farming collective of Sde Boker, which in a decade has created a green, arable plateau from what was a waterless sand-dune, Ben-Gurion took up a new assignment: the tending of the sheep.

Today, he still lives at Sde Boker, occupying a clapboard bungalow and sharing the spare life of the farmers. He no longer shepherds but is writing the history of the Jewish nation from the first wave of Zionist immigrants in the 1870s to the present. He is doing this, he says, so that the younger generation will realize that what has been accomplished up to now is only a beginning, 'and a beginning is not enough!'

*

The text of this book is based on a series of interviews with Ben-Gurion during the filming of the Covenant Communications Corporation production *Forty-Two Six*, the story of his life and times. While the script of *Forty-Two Six* was in preparation Ben-Gurion sat with the production team for a six-hour filmed interview. Cinemascope cameras were transported to the kibbutz from London, technicians brought in from Jerusalem. The library of the Teachers' College of the Negev, an institution which Ben-Gurion helped found and which stands adjacent to Sde Boker itself, was transformed into a studio. Filming occurred for two hour periods on three successive nights, after the heat of the desert sun had abated. Ben-Gurion spoke on a variety of subjects, from his own life to the future of the Jewish People and their mission in Israel. It was his evocation of Isaiah's statement in XLII, 6 of the latter's Biblical Prophecy that the Jews must serve as 'a light unto the nations', a model of wisdom and probity, which inspired the production's title.

The interview constituted a valuable working brief, a measure of authenticity for the concepts presented in *Forty-Two Six*. It also served as 'raw' material for a number of subsidiary projects.

But in its own right, the long exchange with Ben-Gurion stands as a remarkable document. It is a summing-up by a statesman who is also a man of reflection, well aware of shades of meaning and the changing view that time brings of one's own work. It embodies a distillate of thoughts by one who today can review with detachment the events of a long life, the high points of which gave impetus to realizing the two-millennia old Jewish dream of gathering in the exiles and re-building a nation.

What follows is a selection of Ben-Gurion's own words.

THOMAS R. BRANSTEN

1 · The Jews

'I see the man through the cause.' Such is General Moshe Dayan's assessment of Ben-Gurion. The cause is and always has been Israel, a centrifugal core round which the ideas and actions of a totally dedicated personality have revolved. Israel itself in this context is the fulfilment of a militant Jewishness that transcends religion yet derives its vision from Torah, its strength from the fact of Jewish identity.

With the Jews, therefore, with what they are in light of the past and present and with what they seek to be, this account must begin. Here is Ben-Gurion's view of a people he describes as 'difficult unto themselves' but specially called upon by their own prophets to set an example for humanity.

THE Jews are sometimes like the stars, and sometimes they are as dust. I suppose that is true of mankind in general, and of all individuals. Nevertheless, it is what the Talmud specifically says of us. And as a people we do run to extremes.

The best among us have reached very high towards the stars. The worst have fallen exceedingly low because they have had to deny the Jewish ethic which emphasizes moral consciousness and by so doing closes the door on all excuses regarding the portent of one's actions. The traditional Prussian claim to innocence on the grounds of obeying orders is very un-Jewish. For us, right and wrong are between the individual and his own conscience. The Jew who commits evil must, therefore, act in defiance of what his inner being affirms as right. So he carries an extra burden of wickedness.

Moreover, the Jewish moral code unlike the Christian one doesn't tell its adherents 'you should do this or that.' It simply defines what one mustn't do, leaving positive actions to the discretion of each man. The Bible, our Bible which is the Old Testament, makes no injunctions such as: 'Be wise' or 'Be virtuous.' Rather, it cautions that: 'Thou shalt not kill', and 'Thou shalt not covet thy neighbour's wife.' Therefore, to be evil the Jew must go beyond action and transgress against fundamental negatives. That is being wicked indeed.

Equally, to be virtuous it isn't enough merely to avoid evil. One has to take a further step by making a positive contribution to the human condition.

I think this Jewish emphasis on negative rules and positive virtue accounts for a certain drive towards achievement and for a highly developed sense of justice, or rather of injustice. The Jews have always had a tendency to become passionately committed in any spiritual war against injustice, not only when it has concerned them directly but in the name of mankind as a whole. Where there are Jews, there are people fighting man's inhumanity to man, whether this be racial discrimination against the black race in America or intellectual freedom in the Soviet Union (I am thinking specifically of the imprisoned writer Yuri Daniel who has dared to criticize the present regime. There are many of his calibre I could name). Is this not reaching for the stars? I believe so.

Everything we are as Jews, including our drive occasionally to grope beyond traditional bounds, comes directly from the Bible. In size we are nothing as a people and never have been. Had we not been children of the Book, who would have heard of us? We should be lucky to occupy a mere footnote in history. As things stand, a large part of history is our doing. We have never been far removed from the mainstream, often unhappily so and at peril.

I am always astonished at the Jewish contribution to human

thought. So many remarkable thinkers have been Jews. Their work and ideas form vast frames of reference that influence the lives of men everywhere, even when they are not specifically aware of this being so or disagree with the concepts involved. One can loathe or passionately adhere to Marxist doctrine but one cannot deny the impact of Karl Marx's thought on the world. Equally so with Freudianism and Freud.

When I use the star metaphor I am thinking of one who literally bears responsibility for humanity's progress towards them in this century. I mean, of course, Albert Einstein. So far as I know he remains the greatest scientific theoretician of our age. It was my privilege to have had a personal contact with him and, in matters outside the realm of science, to have experienced the nobility of the man.

In Israel to date, we have had no individual who has approached the stars. Such flights of the spirit take time to cultivate. I recall a Frenchman once telling me that it is the job of a thousand years to produce a truly first-class vineyard. Despite our history of four thousand years, our return to Israel is still very recent and we have been too busy struggling merely to survive. In time I have no doubt we shall produce our share of artists and scientists, philosophers and poets.

Yet the very fact of Israel's existence is a notable achievement in which every individual shares. And I do know many Jews here who, because of the circumstances of their lives, are able to lead a more useful existence in terms of their contribution to humanity than their counterparts in the Diaspora.

Regarding virtue and vice, our history in Israel has been a mercurial one. In Isaiah's time our prophets castigated us as the worst people in the world and threatened the loss of the nation. Did our wickedness cost us our homeland? I cannot argue the point after two thousand years. I do know, however, that the regaining of our land was due to an extraordinary act of collective virtue carried out by many thousands at painful sacrifice to themselves and amid the scepticism, even derision, whereby the mass of men, including the Jews, often attempt to deny great undertakings.

The rebirth of Israel was no overnight affair. Nor was it a question of an international legal arrangement. It started in earnest one hundred years ago, in the 1870s when the first pioneers left the relative security of their lives in Eastern Europe and Russia and came here determined to create a Jewish national home on the foundations of the ancient one. Of course, there had always been a Jewish population here and Jewish communities in the area called Palestine. But Israel as a nation was the work of three generations. It continues today, far from complete, especially and in its purest form down in the desert where I live and where we have had to do everything ourselves, from scratch.

But let us return to the intellectual restlessness of the Jews, their long-standing resentment against injustice however abstract or removed from themselves, their almost obsessional drive to search for truth. As I have indicated, these traits are one with the preoccupations of the Bible. For the Bible and for the Jews ever afterwards, both as individuals and as a people, the question of man's mission on earth has been paramount. The answer seems to be in function of what is conceived as man's highest calling, his creativity.

In this respect, the Book of Genesis is most revealing. Christian Gospel begins with the birth of Jesus; the Koran with Mohammed. Torah, however, doesn't start either with Moses or even with Abraham, the original Jew, the man who travelled from Chaldea into unknown territory beyond the Euphrates river thereby becoming a pioneer and the first 'Hebrew' or 'man who crossed over' the river. Torah begins with Creation and we are told that six days after conceiving the light, the grass and all the animals, on the final day of genesis a man and a woman were made and they were in the image of God. Of course, speaking personally as one who is non-religious, I believe that theology reverses the true sequence of events. To me it is clear that God was 'created' in the image of man as the latter's explanation to himself of the mystery of his own earthly presence. More of that in another chapter.

The Bible, taking man as deriving from God, defines Adam as God's surrogate on earth. God surpasses man and the latter cannot even conceive Him as a whole. Yet, we are told, God is the embodiment of love, justice, mercy. When Torah speaks of man being in His image it means he must strive to possess these qualities.

More than all these things, God's most remarkable trait is his creativeness, whence man himself has sprung – according to the Book. Whether he was meant to or not, man from Adam's time has struggled to share in this creativity. This seems to me the crux of the story. God does the impossible, man strives to do the seemingly impossible. He goes to the moon. He also creates a 'land of milk and honey' out of so apparently barren a wilderness as the Negev. This is sharing directly in the adventure of creation.

God also made Eden. But that wasn't so much to man's taste. Man couldn't bear to live in idleness so he contrived to get himself evicted from Paradise and since then has attempted to work his own magic. Often enough he has merely succeeded in creating Hell. Occasionally, and I believe we are doing this here in Israel, he has opened the way to a burgeoning of new life.

From the Bible, therefore, stems Jewish man's concept of himself, an image he has passed on to the whole of western civilization through the daughter religions of Islam and Christianity.

However, the fact that the Book of the Jews came first, before any comparable mode of belief, has its importance to our history. It was for so long unique. For centuries, for millennia it stood as the only ethic that took inspiration not from practical necessities (as did the earlier Hammurabi code, for instance) but from an ideal above and beyond human existence. This accounts both for the richness of the Jewish past and also for many of our troubles. The Book has always constituted a two-edged blessing.

Following the June 1967 war, I wrote a letter to General Charles de Gaulle answering his castigation of the Jews as an 'aggressive' people. I pointed out the obvious fact that no other people has been so exiled, dispersed, hated, persecuted, harried from country to country and finally (in our own time and in supposedly civilized Europe) slaughtered *en masse*. During all this we neither vanished nor despaired nor assimilated but held fast to the conviction that we would some day regain our land.

Are our faith and our suffering unrelated? I think not. One appears to grow from the other. By the metaphysical nature of the Biblical ethic, the Jews developed a universal conscience. That is never a comfortable thing to have, partly because one cannot hope to satisfy such a conscience and it is always nagging, and partly because other men with lesser consciences are constantly being brought up short, with resentment, in their confrontations with such a phenomenon. Jesus, who certainly was afflicted with a universal conscience, found himself on the Roman cross at an early age. The Jews since their exile have suffered perpetual martyrdom.

In their worship of an invisible God, the Jews from their beginnings appeared exotic and thereby menacing to others (one is always afraid of what one doesn't understand). With a code of conduct resolutely loftier and certainly different from that of other men, worshipping a God who was universal and whose very lack of presence carried great authority as evidenced by the seriousness with which the Jews obeyed His injunctions, this small people remained apart. It sought not to evangelize or convert, merely to go its own way, disdainful even in dispersion of its surroundings. Small wonder the Jews never found a true place for themselves outside their own homeland. Small wonder, too, that others looked upon them with an initial distrust often compounded by historical events into more sinister emotions.

If the Bible is one main pillar holding up the Jewish ethos, the other (and equally important one) is nationhood. The uniqueness of the Jewish people and of Judaism consists in this: no other religion is connected with the physical existence of a nation. Remove Jewish history and there is no Judaism.

This explains our attachment to Israel. And to my mind it accounts for the fact that if the Bible stresses creativity, the Jews not as individuals but as Jews were, and only are, truly creative when living in their own land.

What I have called the Jewish ethic, that which we took with us into exile, has certainly been responsible for forming individuals who through the ages have made creative contributions to whatever society they happened to be living in. Those we have already mentioned (Freud, Marx, Einstein and so forth) are cases in point. But Jews as Jews made only one positive contribution. They created through the Talmud and through their traditions a sort of portable homeland that kept them together through two thousand years of wandering and eventually enabled them to return to the very land held by their ancestors.

In exile, the Jews continued to live in their hearts and minds within the bounds of a heritage tied equally to the Bible and to the physical area regarded as home. As I said, this did not endear them to others because they were perpetually different, perpetually a foreign element in any community. But the creative process that produced Torah and that was so much a part of Jewish life before exile largely dried up. It became diverted to custodial duties, to protecting what already existed. The Jews multiplied their interpretations of interpretations, and explanations of the explanations of Scripture. Spiritual life like material life became increasingly impoverished. Jewish life as such shrivelled, went into the cocoon of the ghetto civilization. And if the Jews did happen to produce some creative genius, they were quick to condemn him for 'rocking the boat' as it were. In the seventeenth century, the great philosopher Baruch Spinoza was cast out of the Jewish community. He gave his wisdom to others, not in Hebrew but in a foreign tongue. The Jews lived in political, economic and spiritual isolation. It was only by the renewal of practical interest in the homeland a century ago that the Jews found scope once again for their creative power as a people.

It follows, therefore, that without a Jewish national community, without Israel, there can be no truly creative Jewish life.

Even with the best of intentions, the Jew in the Diaspora can never be exclusively a Jew, and in fact he's a Jew very little. Whether they recognize it or not, Diaspora Jews live in a permanent 'condition of exile'. I mean that they are always a minority and thus dependent on a majority beyond their capacity to control. They are torn in never-ending conflict between a desire to preserve their Jewish status, which keeps them separate, and the assimilationist pressures of the social structure. In the Diaspora, very few Jews are among those elements of the population that furnish the basic labour of society, the farmers and industrial workers. Most Jews live crowded together in the cities. Even in the United States, where the Jews form a generally prosperous community and where there is certainly no restriction of movement, they are concentrated in the six largest cities, along the Eastern sea-board, in Chicago and in Los Angeles on the West Coast. Of a population of six million, almost three million live in the greater New York area alone.

In poorer countries, the gathering of Jews in the main cities makes them economically and physically vulnerable. The recent killing of Jewish hostages in Baghdad and the continuing persecution of the city's ancient Jewish community show how readily the authorities are able to sweep down upon these people, gathered in upon themselves, huddled in a central part of the city, ripe at any moment for persecution.

Whether living in poverty, overcrowded in ghettos, or in wealth still gathered in the cities, Jews in the Diaspora have remained separate from the primary sources of vitality of any people: the soil and the factories. Thus basically, no matter how comfortably off, they have lacked solid ground under their feet.

Let us take the example I know best, the Diaspora's most successful community. I am thinking of the American Jewish community with which I have had the most personal experience. I once lived in the United States for three years and I have had to travel there often to deal with its representatives.

We in Israel have a special link with American Jewry which has contributed so generously to our efforts. We are of course grateful – more than grateful.

We know also that as people, the Jews of the United States do very useful, important work in their own country and are represented in all the professions. American literature owes a big debt to Jews, especially in the twentieth century. So do the arts in general as do the law, politics and the sciences. Nevertheless, even in the United States the Jews have comparatively little representation in heavy industry, high finance, in the proletariat or in agriculture. They are not a basic element of the national economy.

Further, a Jew in America is a split person. Or, more precisely, when is he a Jew? Some are Jews one day a year, for Yom Kippur or the Day of Atonement, the holiest day of the Jewish calendar occurring on the tenth day of the seventh month, when one fasts and prays for forgiveness of sin. On that day the synagogues are full. Other Americans attend regularly every Saturday or sometimes on Sunday as a concession to the general, non-Jewish habits of the country. Perhaps a Jew will belong to a community centre which makes him feel he is participating in a Jewish activity, or one involving other Jews. Certainly, he can often be counted on to contribute generously to Israel since Americans are a generous people.

Nine-tenths of the time, however, the Jew in the United States is living the life of any other American. And so he should be in American terms. But not in Jewish terms. And what are his activities? He lives in a house. The odds are strong that the house wasn't built by Jews. He uses electricity but it is not being created by Jews as such. He uses a bus or subway which certainly weren't made by Jews. And even if they were, it would have no significance in the context of America. The house, the subway, the electricity are American commodities whether used by Jew or non-Jew. This is neither good nor bad, it's just a fact.

Most of the time, then, even the observant Jew is living as a non-Jew. At worst, his Jewishness is held against him, minimal though it be; at best, it counts for little in his daily life.

The conclusion is simple. Jews should come to Israel. In the Diaspora they cannot really be Jews without an artificial self-consciousness and tension that disappears completely from their lives once they arrive here. Outside Israel, the end result for a Jew inevitably is either the ghetto or assimilation. Within Israel it is as natural to be Jewish as it is to be French in France, Greek in Greece and so on. Even the United States is not really the exception it appears to be. Jews as Jews, if they do not totally assimilate into the famous American 'melting pot' (and they are free to do so), are still a minority. Certain doors are closed to them. They represent a special interest group. Naturally enough, their offspring have every interest in disappearing without trace into the community as a whole.

In Israel, the Jew needn't be confronted with such arbitrary problems and he needn't disappear. Here, the condition of Jewishness, whether a man is religious or not, informs the environment. It is part of the natural setting. The individual contributes to that setting with his every gesture. So he can live the complete life, being a hundred per cent Jewish while he is simultaneously a hundred per cent a human being in society, with no conflict.

This is a purely Jewish reason for coming to Israel. We offer a full Jewish life and a full human life, which, if not richer economically than elsewhere, promises greater spiritual fulfilment.

There are other reasons for immigrating which I shall discuss later. But for a Jew, the life here contains the hope of rich moral satisfaction.

I have always thought this and it has shaped my own attitude towards Israel. I came here very young, when the idea of a nation was characterized by most Jews as wild fantasy. How vividly I recall, as a fresh immigrant, my long walks through the countryside and my dreams of seeing the land become a Jewish nation once more. I used to walk a great deal and I've pretty well covered the north and central areas on foot. There was always a reason for taking to the road. A political meeting in Haifa, a Hebrew Society gathering in Jerusalem, a festival at a farming collective, all sorts of occasions here and there that I wanted to attend. And in those days, one went on foot or on horseback. I didn't have a horse or the money for one, so I walked.

One day, I remember coming down from the farming community of Zirkon Yacov above Haifa to Jaffa for a meeting. It took two days of continuous travel through what is now the heartland of Israel, its most settled, built-up and cultivated area. I was so tired when I arrived in Jaffa that for the only time in my life I slept through for twenty-four hours. Well, the country was very sparsely settled then. This was in 1908. The Jewish villages, the new ones established to cultivate the land, numbered less than twenty. I had arrived in 1906 and since then not a single Jewish community had been added to the existing number. There were some pioneers in the Galilee. But they were preparing the land for permanent settlements and we needed people to put down roots throughout the country. I recall hearing the welcome news a year or so later that another settlement was being built. It was the first one in my time and consisted of only six houses near Tiberias, all owned by five brothers. Small as this was, it seemed a vindication of our faith.

Walking through the barren plain, seeing only an occasional tribe of nomadic Bedouins (they still roam the country at will, largely impervious both to civilization and politics) and a few poverty-stricken Arab villages, I was sure even then that this land would become entirely Jewish. I knew we had here the ideal opportunity to prove our mettle and ourselves as Jews. There was nothing here. It was literally a forgotten corner of the Turkish Empire and of the globe. Nobody wanted it, certainly not the Palestinian Arabs who were placidly vegetating in their poverty under the Turks. Their subsequent indignation at the Jewish presence was fomented artificially by special interest groups and the propaganda machines of the surrounding Arab nations. Were the Jews to disappear from Israel, which they won't, one thing is sure. The Arabs of Palestine would have no chance for autonomy given the expansionism of Egypt, Syria, Jordan and, to a lesser degree, Lebanon. Of that one can be certain!

In any event, when I came here, no one could have cared less about the place. Anyone was free to come and create afresh.

I believed then, as I do today, that we held a clear title to this country. Not the right to take it away from others (there were no others), but the right and the duty to fill its emptiness, restore life to its barrenness, to re-create a modern version of our ancient nation. And I felt we owed this effort not only to ourselves but to the land as well.

This country has passed through many hands. It has been conquered incessantly and incessantly abandoned. It has known the Egyptians, Assyrians, Babylonians, Persians, Greeks, Romans, Arabs, Seljukes, the Crusaders, Mamelukes, Ottoman Turks and the British, apart from ourselves and the Canaanites before us. The Canaanites exist no more. Other than they and the Jews, the land has never been a home to anyone. It has been a battlefield, conquered territory, a place to plunder, a crossroads or a grazing ground. Only the Jews have loved the land for itself, have worked it, improved it, made it theirs through their care for it. This was true two thousand years ago, it is equally true today. Israel is ours in the twentieth century not because we fought wars over it (these were protective actions after the fact of our presence) but because we settled it. I have devoted my life to the act of settling this land. And as I walked through it in 1906 and 1908, I knew our labour would prevail and that one day the country would be ours.

As a corollary to the establishment of Israel, I see the re-birth of Hebrew as the Jewish national language as a great victory and a great affirmation of our link to our ancient past. The languages of exile, principally Yiddish and Ladino, are perhaps interesting in their cultural and folkloric significance. But they are languages of humiliation. Hebrew, and with it the knowledge of its greatest written works, Torah and Talmud, are the matrix in which Jewishness is embedded. These elements kept the Jews true to themselves in dispersion. Today, Hebrew in modern guise gives the nation of Israel a special distinctiveness and acts as a constant reminder of the historical heritage from which our national life derives its richness.

Outside Israel, the growth of secularism brings the Jewish communities of the world ever closer to assimilation. Secularism is a fact of our time and since I am not religious I have no reason to deplore it. But if I'm for secularism, I'm certainly not for the ignorance that comes in its wake.

In areas where Jews are not persecuted, an increasingly high number vanish, not dramatically but passively, passing into an anonymity born of lack of conviction. Were it not for Israel's existence, we should have to resign ourselves to total assimilation within the next century. A great cultural and humanistic tradition would be lost to mankind and the Jews never would have fulfilled Isaiah's command to act as 'a light unto the nations'.

Fortunately, with Israel's presence assured, there is no danger of this happening. But even within this country secularism threatens knowledge and ignorance threatens lack of interest in the essentials of the Jewish tradition. The problem becomes increasingly acute for the velocity of history grows as our technological powers augment. The world has changed in the past one hundred years more than it did in the preceeding thousand. And the momentum continues to be cumulative.

It is all the more urgent, therefore, for Jews everywhere to realize their affinity with Israel, the Bible and Hebrew, the pillars whereon the condition of being Jewish rests.

How to make this realization come about? I think the answer today is the same one we had in 1906 and in 1870: pioneering.

Pioneers are open to the accusation of being rebels, of not accepting any mode of 'normal' life since that would be too conformist. But what exactly do we mean by the term normal life? Isn't it usually taken to describe a state of inertia where all is calm? Surely that sort of normality is highly abnormal! Life, after all, is struggle. The best tool with which to combat an assimilationism born of apathy is more of the spirit that built this country.

The pioneers I joined during my first years in Israel were poor. We wore what clothing we could find and our hair was long because we had neither time nor the facilities to cut it. But we weren't necessarily nonconformist for its own sake. We wanted to create a new life, go beyond the life that already existed.

That need has remained with me ever since. I think it found its highest expression fifteen years ago when I came to the desert. The Negev is even a more dramatic challenge right now, in our time, than the pioneering of earlier days.

As to the future, if the spirit of Israel is to endure, pioneering must go on. That is another reason why Jews should come here. Not only so that they can live wholly integrated lives but to render service. We don't need newcomers in the cities where there are enough people – more than enough! We need them here, in the desert, making a fertile land from sand

and rock with the help of modern science, coupled to the sweat of our backs.

Pioneering is Israel's life blood, as it is the life blood of all mankind. Going to the moon and coming to the desert to plant saplings are similar acts, in my opinion. Man must reach for the stars, it is in his nature. We have seen that the Bible first defined this aspect of human existence. But the stars are only a symbol. There is much to do on earth. The Jews today have the opportunity missed by so many generations in exile. They can follow the prophets who demanded that Israel be two things: that it represent a covenant between all the Jews so as to strengthen their cohesion as a people and that its mission also be to act as an example, 'a light unto the nations', for all mankind. For me, pioneering is setting the example and there can be no higher Jewish ideal than creating from this bare, besieged little land a rich and enduring way of life that in its plenitude will never stop searching for new areas of endeavour but that will serve as a model to inspire humanity everywhere.

2·Early Years

David Ben-Gurion grew up as David Gryn, fourth child of the lawyer Avigdor Gryn who occupied a wooden house on the Street of Goats. This was an unpaved often muddy lane in the Jewish quarter of Plonsk, a small market city some forty miles northwest of Warsaw. Here David Gryn was born on 16 October 1886. The region is now Poland but then it was under Russian Tsarist occupation.

Today, no Jews live in Plonsk. Their once extensive cemetery is a weed-infested lot marked only by a few cracked gravestones that the State road-builders could find no use for. Three of the four synagogues have disappeared, the fourth remains as a granary. All this testifies to the efficiency of Nazi extermination and to the policies of the Nazis' successors. But at the turn of the century millions of Jews were settled in Poland and every town had its populous Jewish community. Under Russian, German or Austro-Hungarian rule, depending on the region, the Jews shared with the Poles themselves the unhappy status of second-class citizen.

Plonsk, however, was a backwater where even Jews could hope to live out their days in peace, relatively free from the threat of sudden pogrom or expulsion. Here, David Gryn spent childhood and adolescence until, at the age of nineteen, he left for Palestine to work as a Zionist pioneer for the revival of the Jewish National Home. This is what he says of his early life and of his awakening to the call of Israel.

I can hardly remember a time when the idea of building what we used to call 'Eretz Israel', or the Land of Israel, wasn't the guiding factor of my life. It is no exaggeration to say that at three I had daydreams of coming to Palestine. And certainly from my tenth year on, I never thought of spending my life anywhere else.

The events of my childhood influenced me very naturally in this direction. In my third year, my grandfather began teaching me Hebrew. He would sit me on his knee and I would repeat words after him. Within a few months, I became quite fluent, actually learning to speak and to love the Jews' ancient tongue before I could read in any language (Yiddish and Russian were the basic languages of our community. Hebrew was considered by all but a small minority of the highly educated as a 'dead' vehicle of Talmud and Torah, to be struggled through in school and then forgotten). Listening to grandfather telling stories of Jewish history, I clearly recall thinking to myself: 'Plonsk isn't my real home. Here we live among strangers. I must go the Land of Israel.'

When I was just a little older, Theodor Herzl came to our small city. An Austrian Jew and a journalist, Herzl had been so stricken by the anti-Semitism of the Dreyfus affair in France that he wrote a book, *The Jewish State*, which called for the founding of a Jewish nation. He devoted the remainder of his life to starting the modern Zionist movement. When he appeared in Plonsk, people greeted him as the Messiah. Everyone went around saying 'The Messiah has come', and we children were much impressed. It was easy for a small boy to see in Herzl the Messiah. He was a tall, finely featured man whose impressive black beard flowed wide down to his chest. One glimpse of him and I was ready to follow him then and there to the land of my ancestors.

My generation was ripe for Zionism. Our parents were content to dream and talk while making their peace with the unstable but not at that time actively hostile environment of Eastern Europe. My father, a lawyer and a prominent member of the Jewish community (though some disapproved of him for his free-thinking ideas), called himself a 'Lover of Zion'. Before Herzl, he and his friends would meet frequently at our house and one would hear repeated over and over the phrase 'The Land of Israel'. Later, the group incorporated itself into the Zionist Movement. In that time and place the entire atmosphere, not only for me but for all the Jews of my age in Europe northeast of the Danube, favoured the idea of taking matters to the logical conclusion: emigration and active building of Eretz Israel rather than mere talk, dreams or passive waiting for the magic fulfilment of prophecies. In such a sense, Herzl was indeed like a Messiah since he galvanized the feeling of the youth that Eretz Israel was achievable. He added, however, that it could only come to pass if we built it with our own hands.

This was a concept bitterly opposed by many of our elders and especially by religious sects such as the Chassidim who felt it was impious to anticipate mystic promises of heavenly recall to The Land.

The Jewish community of Plonsk consisted of three elements. The poor were small merchants, shopkeepers, peddlars. My own family belonged to the middle or professional group, neither rich nor poor, but comfortably off. From this social level came the intellectuals, the freethinkers, socialists, scholars and Zionists. The Chassidim, mostly prosperous, considered themselves an elite and to prove it lived slightly apart from the rest of us. They attended their own synagogue, kept to themselves. Only two of their number became Zionists at the time the movement was sweeping our part of the Jewish world. The rest thundered against Zionism's activist philosophy and forced the two converts to leave town hastily. Whenever any Jew departed for Palestine, the Chassidim sat Shiva for seven days as though he had died.

What about anti-Semitism in all this? For my generation, it played only an indirect role in our desire to emigrate.

Certainly anti-Semitism had acted as a catalyst on Zionism in general. It had turned Herzl himself from a dilettante, a darling of Vienna's literary salons and perfectly at home in the non-Jewish world, into a man dedicated to the cause of a homeland. And the fact that Jews were subject to periodic ostracism and persecution made it all the more obviously imperative for them to have a place of their own.

Yet for many of us, anti-Semitic feeling had little to do with our dedication. I personally never suffered anti-Semitic persecution. Plonsk was remarkably free of it, or at least the Jews felt well protected in the cocoon of their community life. Nevertheless, and I think this very significant, it was Plonsk that sent the highest proportion of Jews to Eretz Israel from any town in Poland of comparable size. We emigrated not for negative reasons of escape but for the positive purpose of rebuilding a homeland, a place where we wouldn't be perpetual strangers and that through our toil would become irrevocably our own.

Life in Plonsk was peaceful enough. There were three main communities: Russians, Jews and Poles. Each lived apart from the others. The Russians as the occupiers kept a firm hand on the civil administration. There were no Polish or Jewish officials. Officials or police almost never interfered in dealings between the Jewish and Polish communities. They disliked both equally and took an aloof attitude to the town's day-to-day life.

The number of Jews and Poles in the city were roughly equal, about five thousand each. The Jews, however, formed a compact, centralized group occupying the innermost districts whilst the Poles were more scattered, living in outlying areas and shading off into the peasantry. Consequently, when a gang of Jewish boys met a Polish gang the latter would almost inevitably represent a single suburb and thus be poorer in fighting potential than the Jews who even if their numbers were initially fewer could quickly call on reinforcements from the entire quarter. Far from being afraid of them, they were rather afraid of us. In general, however, relations were amicable, though distant.

I must add that my father maintained very friendly ties with numbers of Polish people who consulted him profession-ally and who, on many occasions, indicated their trust in him. That didn't mean the population at large wasn't anti-Semitic. Most Poles, as devout Catholics, looked upon Jews as 'the murderers of Christ'. That this view had no basis in fact, historical or apocryphal, meant little. But ingrained anti-Semitism didn't prevent Poles and Russians from having their particular Jewish friends. I'm reminded of a story con-cerning a former mayor of Vienna during the late nineteenth century who was known as a notorious anti-Semite. Never-theless, he cultivated the society of more than a few Jews. When someone took him up on this apparent contradiction he retorted: 'In Vienna, I decide who is a Jew!'

Because of my Zionism I had little interest in learning the local languages. I felt they had no relevance to my life as I wouldn't be staying. I did acquire Russian and read widely in the literature, particularly Dostoyevsky and Tolstoy. I was so impressed by one of Tolstoy's heroes that at the age of eight I announced to my family I was a vegetarian, a phase that didn't last very long.

During my school years, I read mainly Russian literature and Jewish history. When I was about nine, two books made an impression on me that has lasted throughout my life. The first was *Ahavatzion* by Abraham Mapu, the originator of the modern Hebrew novel. The other was *Uncle Tom's Cabin*, which I read in Russian translation. Mapu first instilled in me an understanding of life in Biblical times. We of course learned the Bible in Shule. But there it was dry and remote. Mapu made it live. He described real people leading lives that I as an inhabitant of Plonsk and of what was nearly the twentieth century could comprehend. And Mapu's characters spoke the language of the Bible, which through his pen became once again a living language. Mapu makes a point of describing

life in the times of the Jewish Kings, the Biblical period and
not the Talmudic one of exile. There was very little else
available to a boy that re-created the times of ancient Judah
and Israel so vividly – thus putting the dream of starting anew
into a context of everyday reality.

Uncle Tom's Cabin stirred me for different reasons. I was
taken aback by the idea of slavery, that a man could exploit
other men so crudely, Tom's innate nobility impressed me
deeply. Slavery neither crushed him nor took away his
humanity. It was easy to draw the parallel between his tale
and the story of Moses who repudiated slavery for the first
time in recorded history.

Dreams of Eretz Israel seemed most impractical for me
personally during my childhood, for physically I was very
frail. The doctors said I must gain strength in the country. I
have always remembered with an emotion bordering on awe
the act of devotion my mother made for me at that time. She
was a simple woman, attached to her home, deeply observant
and ill at ease beyond the confines of our own community.
Yet she took me to live in a country village, surrounded by
people whom she feared and whose ways were alien to her.
Mother expected great things of me. When I was nine, a
physician made a phrenological examination of my head, very
much the medical fashion of the day, and predicted I would
become a remarkable man. She was very happy to hear this
and said: 'My Duchka (this was my diminutive name when
I was a child) will be a great rabbi. And he will upset people!'

My father, as I have said, wasn't devout. He did observe
religious practice. But essentially he was a freethinker. Many
years later, in 1925, he came to Eretz Israel and there dropped
all religious observances. But when as a boy I suddenly
declared my disbelief in God, father was very stern with me
and insisted I go through the rituals of belief for the sake of
being at one with the community.

When I was ten my mother died. For a long time, several
years, life seemed to have lost all meaning. I continued school

and my reading but with barrenness in my heart. I was obsessed by a feeling of human futility. Then, when I was fourteen, I suddenly emerged from this tunnel to throw myself heart and soul into the Zionist movement.

With two older boys, Shmuel Fuchs and Shlomo Zemach (the latter became one of the finest Israeli writers of my time), I helped establish a group to teach Hebrew. We called it the Ezra Society after the great teacher who returned to Jerusalem from Babylon to rebuild the Temple. There seemed to us marked affinity between Ezra's mission and time and our own newly born hopes for Palestine.

I joined Zemach in teaching Hebrew to the poor. All children went to Cheder but the poor, as is usually the case, for one reason and another received the thin end of the cultural heritage. Our activities met with success and we expanded operations by having the first pupils teach others. We went through the Jewish quarter teaching Hebrew to our contemporaries until the entire youth had a feel for the language. Then, the younger generation took on their parents and soon Plonsk was one of the few cities of the Diaspora where almost every family had basic fluency in Hebrew.

A year or so after organizing the Ezra Society I began dividing my time between Plonsk and Warsaw. There was no secondary or high school in the area near my home and I had decided to prepare to study engineering at the Warsaw Polytechnic Academy. I knew engineers would be needed to build up backward and undeveloped Palestine. Besides, my father insisted that I attend university and finish my education before thinking about emigration. He even wrote to Herzl asking his help in finding me a place in a faculty of Western Europe, preferably Vienna or Basel. I didn't know this at the time nor at any point during my father's life. He never once mentioned it to me. Years later, the letter turned up among documents in the Zionist museum of Jerusalem. That is how it came to my attention. Whether Herzl answered or not I have no way of knowing. I doubt it. He was pretty busy at the time running the gamut of the Chanceries of Europe.

In any case, during the year 1904 my plans changed abruptly. Many Zionists, including Herzl, opted for settling not in Palestine but in Uganda. Middle European Jewish youth was very much against the Uganda proposal and determined to fight it with every available means. The only true weapon was immediate departure for Palestine in the name of Eretz Israel.

The first to go from Plonsk was my friend and fellow Hebrew teacher of the Ezra Society, Zemach. He was several years older than the rest of us. He also had the personal reason of wishing to get away from an oppressive family situation. It was decided he would go for a year or so, then return to report to us firsthand at home. His departure was quite an affair. Zemach came from an old and scholarly family. But very poor. Then, his father won five hundred roubles in a lottery. The boy was given the money to bank in a neighbouring town. He took two hundred roubles from the sum to pay for his passage to Palestine. He was so ashamed of what he had done that he didn't return home but fled straight to Warsaw where he hid in my room waiting for the date of his journey to arrive.

I knew his father would come looking for him and that I would be one of the first persons he would visit. Two fellow students took Zemach to their quarters. Soon after that, his father appeared at my door. 'Where is Shlomo?' he demanded. I said: 'He is going to Eretz Israel and I cannot take you to him.' We argued back and forth but then suddenly the old man broke down and began to weep for his son. I couldn't stand seeing him cry that way. So I said: 'If you promise not to prevent his going then I will send for him.' His father swore he would abide by this and the two were re-united. But Zemach wasn't easy in his conscience until he could repay the two hundred roubles he had taken, even though his father pressed them upon him. It was the first thing he thought of doing upon his return a year and a half later.

Throughout his first visit to Palestine, Zemach wrote to me faithfully every week. Long, detailed letters of twenty-five pages and more. I could hardly wait for them to arrive. He would tell me of his hardships in getting a job, the kind of work he did when he could find any, how he was taking to his new life of manual labour, what the country looked like, in what state he had found the various groups of pioneers already there and what were the burning issues in their discussions on labour and Zionist ideology. He wrote of the harsh realities of the pioneering life, so far removed from our rosy, visionary dreams as youngsters in Plonsk. The problems, difficult and numerous, he never sought to conceal. Yet there was no hint of despair in these eloquent communications. He always had suggestions as to what must be done to overcome the troubles at hand.

Thanks to Zemach's letters, I came to feel I knew Palestine as well as I knew the land of my birth. I could visualize every feature of the regions he visited, and every aspect of the physical, social, political climate of the land. Those letters were my most precious possession during all my early years. I hoped someday to see them published. What a fine record they would have made of the pioneering life! Unfortunately, in the First World War when the Turks expelled many Jews from Palestine, they were lost along with all the personal effects I had in Jerusalem.

Zemach returned to Plonsk in the summer of 1906 and this time I would not be restrained from going back to Palestine with him. University, my father's ambitions for me, the professional advantages of a higher education, all these considerations meant little in terms of getting to grips with the land itself. In Warsaw, in Europe, I felt I was marking time. I was growing older without coming closer to my goal. Zionism wasn't a talking point or a dream. It was reality. But only if one followed through and went to Palestine with the purpose of picking up a shovel and creating Eretz Israel. For nearly two thousand years, the Jews in exile had loved their land from afar. In the mind they had cherished the words of the Prophets telling them that someday they would return. Well, the time was now. And if God created the universe we at least could plant fruit trees in the Galilee's rocky soil.

Such feelings pushed me to hesitate no longer. I broke the news to my father who was dismayed. I persevered and Zemach and I planned our trip. Then, less than a week before we were due to board the train for the port of Odessa on the Black Sea, I was arrested.

This was my second experience of police and prison. In Warsaw, I had already been picked up by a policeman who considered that my hair was too long. I suppose it made me look the stereotype of an anarchist. In those days, almost three-quarters of a century ago, we had similar problems to the youth of today. As the French say, the more things change, the more they remain the same! Anyway, my father was summoned to the capital to bail me out. When he presented his visiting card to the chief of the police station, it transpired they both had the same name. 'You're Avigdor Gryn? I too am Avigdor Gryn,' the policeman said. The two men shook hands and I was released.

The second arrest was far more serious. It came about because the rabbis of the Plonsk area were in the habit of using me as a secular mediator in some of the local semi-legal problems that cropped up in the Jewish community. The Jews avoided Russian courts, whenever they possibly could. When legal troubles arose, they went to the rabbi who often turned over routine affairs to a mediator for preliminary elucidation. If the thing could be settled without going further and without involving the rabbi as the highest Jewish authority, then so much the better. I enjoyed this activity and the rabbis had confidence in my ability although I was only fifteen when I began mediating. I must say I never lost an opportunity to militate for Zionism. I recall one case, for instance, in which a couple were having a row over a dowry. They wanted a divorce and I ruled that before obtaining it the husband should return his wife's dowry money of seven hundred roubles. But I said to her: 'You may keep six hundred roubles. One hundred you should give to the Zionist Committee.' She readily agreed.

I was arrested and thrown in jail while attempting to resolve a quarrel between two rabbis in a village near Plonsk. The Russians heard of the dispute and for some unclear reason decided to make an issue of this particular event to underline the all-pervading nature of their administrative authority. The local Commissar intervened without warning, accusing me of attempting to disrupt Russian justice. The police confiscated my papers and talked ominously of sending me to Siberia. That would have ruined my plans for Palestine for years to come. By the time I emerged, I could have looked ahead to long years of military service in the Tsarist army.

I was desperate. Luckily, I managed to smuggle word to the Zionist Committee in Warsaw. It responded quickly and magnificently, spending a thousand roubles on persuading various officials to return my papers and let me free. In a dazed and shaken mood, I managed to catch the train for Odessa.

While waiting there for a ship to Jaffa, Zemach and I visited the famous Zionist leader Menahem Ussishkin. We had plans for bringing Jewish youth from Eastern Europe to Palestine on a large scale. Ussishkin received us in a manner that opened my eyes to the dangers of theoretical Zionism. He was cold and uncordial. He told us the Turkish government didn't want mass immigration and said it was necessary first to send doctors and agricultural engineers to prepare the way. He seemed most put out that Zemach and I should think of immigrating without consulting his committee. The interview was brief and as we left his office he shouted after us: 'Do you want to die of malaria?' The occasion left me with a life-long aversion towards people who talk rather than act.

We shipped on a Russian freighter, travelling fourth class and sleeping on deck. We did not mind the filth, bad fare or the hardship for we knew that in just fourteen days we would be anchoring in Jaffa.

3·Pioneering

JAFFA when I first arrived was a bitter disappointment. All the previous night, Zemach and I had stood at the ship's rail gazing at the shore of Palestine as we steamed slowly southward from the Lebanon. I could hardly wait to step onto the soil of the homeland. But when I did, the circumstances took me aback.

Today, this little town is only a fishing port and a suburb of modern Tel-Aviv (which didn't come into being until the 1920s). In 1906, however, Jaffa was the chief gateway into Palestine from the West. Since the country was a forgotten corner of Earth, the gateway was modest enough! But poor and rundown though it was with only one main street lined with stalls and small shops, the town certainly didn't lack colour. The narrow, cobbled alleyways off the main avenue were brimming with people of many origins: Turkish, French and English traders; Armenian shopkeepers; Arab dockworkers, guides, beggars; an occasional Catholic or Greek Orthodox monk; missionaries representing a variety of faiths; a few Jews some of whose families had lived there since the time of King Saul. The Zionist Committee had an office in Jaffa. So did several Jewish political organizations which maintained hostels to welcome their fellow immigrants while seeking to enlist them into whatever group or cause they represented.

As I stepped off the gangway, two men pushed through the crowd. One grabbed Zemach and the other hustled me away in a different direction. Next thing I knew, I was standing in the room of a seedy inn being harangued by ten or twelve young men gathered round a bottle of brandy. Between swigs of alcohol, they held forth on Marxist philosophy, roundly denouncing the theory of historical materialism. Turning to me aggressively, they demanded my views. I had listened for a few moments in confusion, getting my bearings. But now I felt anger rising. Here I had come to build Eretz Israel and first thing, after a long journey, after turning my back on education and my father's hopes for me, after finally arriving in the land of my ancestors, I was being asked to pronounce on Marxism. I burst out: 'Go to hell with your historical materialism. I've come to Eretz Israel and you talk to me of theories. What sort of Jews can you be?' And I stormed out slamming the door.

Then and there, I decided that Jaffa was no place for me. After locating Zemach, who had extricated himself from a rival outfit, I set out on foot with him for Petach Tikvah, the oldest Jewish farming settlement in the country and a three hour walk slightly inland to the north.

At Petach Tikvah (in English, 'The Door of Hope') I felt I had finally arrived. We came to the gates at dusk and with our small reserve of money bought some simple food. Then we lay down in a field near the road to sleep.

That first night in Palestine sleep refused to come. I kept thinking about all that had happened and saying to myself: 'Here I am in a Hebrew village of the Holy Land.' I wrote of that night in a letter to my father:

The howling of the jackals in the vineyards the braying of donkeys in the stables, the croaking of frogs in the ponds, the heavy scent of acacias, the sound of the sea in the distance, the shadows of the orange trees in the half-light, the stars twinkling in a dark blue sky that glistened and seemed unreal, everything was so wonderfully strange as in some legendary realm. I thought of all the stages of my journey, the farewells, the sea passage and the approach to the coast of Palestine. And now I was in Eretz Israel. Was it really true? I sat up all night communing with these new skies . . .

The sky was wonderful. But the rocky land yielded little. I knew from Zemach's earlier letters how hard it was to get work. Now I found out for myself that even to survive would take all the energy and ingenuity I possessed.

The Jewish farmers from whom I sought hire as a day labourer were the sons of pioneers. The example of their fathers back in the 1870s and 1890s had done much to inspire my generation. Those were the men of the First Aliyah, or 'first wave' of modern immigrants. We were the Second Aliyah. I recall the effect upon me of a letter from one of the older generation appearing in a book of *Memoirs* of pioneering days that I still possess. The letter was from a man named Ze'ev Dubnow and was written in 1882 in answer to his brother, a well-known Russian Jewish historian, Simeon Dubnow. Simeon as elder brother and head of the family had demanded that Ze'ev stop his 'ridiculous folly' of trying to 'find himself' as a labourer in Palestine, an activity that Simeon considered madness. His brother, he admonished, should return to St. Petersburg where the family lived and take up respectable work as a university lecturer. Ze'ev wrote back:

Do you really think, my dear brother, that my sole purpose in coming here was to 'find' myself? That if I did find myself I would have achieved my aim and that if I didn't I would deserve pity? No! My ultimate aim, like the aim of many others, is great, wide, unlimited. But not incapable of realization. The ultimate aim is to build up this land of Israel and restore to the Jews the political independence that has been taken from them for the past two thousand years. Don't laugh. This is no dream. The means of achieving it can be the setting up of villages for agriculture and crafts, the building of factories and their gradual expansion, in other words a total effort to transfer all employment and agriculture into Jewish hands. In addition, it will be necessary to train young people and the young generations of the future in the use of firearms (in the wild and free Turkish Empire anything is possible) and then . . . then even I give myself up to reveries. Then will come that glorious day of which Isaiah prophesied in his glowing message of comfort. The Jews, with weapons in their hands if necessary, will announce with a loud voice that they are masters in their ancient land. It doesn't matter that this wonderful day will come only in fifty years or later. What is fifty years for such an undertaking?

Thus spoke the First Aliyah, inspiring the hopes of the Second. But in Palestine times had changed. The old pioneers, the first modern rebuilders of Zion who had stuck to their ideal in the face of tremendous travail and suffering, had mostly died off. I'm afraid the majority of their sons, heirs to their land and agricultural experience, did not carry on in the same spirit. The offspring of men like Ze'ev Dubnow felt they had already accomplished enough in making a living from the soil. Moreover, they were repelled by young newcomers like myself with our raggedy clothes, long hair and outspoken talk of socialism, collective living and the sharing of wealth. We talked much, but in the eyes of our prospective employers our capacity for farm work, our physical stamina in the face of poor diet, relentless heat, malaria and the back-breaking tasks required to cultivate that arid, unyielding land impressed them little. We frightened them with theories and annoyed them with our lack of farming competence. They turned their backs on us, preferring Arab workers who were more efficient, demanded less pay and, most of all, didn't presume to social equality with the employer.

At Petach Tikvah, I literally starved. I was small and frail looking which made my personal ability to find any job at all highly precarious. Every day, hundreds of Arabs would walk into the fields and vineyards to begin the chores. The young Jews would gather near the synagogue hoping a farmer would come by. If one did, he would feel each candidate's arm to determine whether there was sufficient muscle for the work. My arms being of the pipestem variety at the time – they rapidly grew in girth when I became a pioneer a year later – I would usually be passed by with a glance. It took me ten days to get my first assignment. Then it was the lesser task of carting wheelbarrows of manure for spreading in the orange groves.

For this I received the equivalent of 2½d. a day, worth rather more than nowadays but still a wage that would only pay for a minimum diet.

With life at Petach Tikvah so uncertain, I wandered from settlement to settlement, my clothes in tatters, my body on the edge of breakdown from famine. I stayed a few weeks on the plateau of Kfar Saba and spent another period in the vineyards of Rishon-Le-Zion where I planted vines, shifted manure, dug irrigation ditches, ploughed, helped carry away the endless rocks and boulders that plagued all attempts to farm this earth.

Then the weather changed abruptly, without transition at all, from boiling heat to a cold drizzle that betokened winter. The land turned to mud. My clothing was inadequate and so was my diet. I quickly succumbed to malaria.

The attacks came every ten days or so and during them I couldn't move, let alone work. My temperature would go up to about 104°F and I was often delirious. This went on for three or four days, then the fever would subside, leaving me weak and shaken. I became quite philosophical about this cycle and knew when the sickness would hit me. I recall one occasion when I felt an attack coming. Work was scarce and I spent my last coppers on a *pita*, a large, flat loaf of unleavened Arab bread. I nibbled at it trying to make it last through the day. I was hungrier than I had reckoned and by three in the afternoon the *pita* had dwindled to a crumb. 'Well', I thought to myself, 'it doesn't matter. I won't be hungry until this evening and then I can sleep.' But when I lay down and closed my eyes, I had a terrible vision of chickens roasting on a spit and dripping hot fat onto piles of bread. I was in agony. On the one hand, I felt exhausted with malaria. On the other, whenever I began to doze off I contemplated those lines of simmering chickens that I knew my hands could never reach.

A doctor whom a friend called in to attend me during one malaria bout said I would never shake the disease and that for me staying in Palestine meant death. I had better go back to Europe and be quick about it, he told me. My well-meaning friends all pointed out that this was hardly a disgrace. Half the immigrants who came to Palestine in those early days took one look and caught the same ship home again. Already, I could call myself a veteran.

Of course, I didn't listen to any of them. I hung on grimly trying to let the disease and the lack of food hinder me as little as possible in the course I had determined my life should take. I wrote to my father: 'There is no going back to the old life. Zionism is a struggle and one can only feel sorry for those who flee the battlefield blaming conditions here.' One of the returnees to Plonsk must have reported my plight to my father. He wrote begging me to come home and sent me ten roubles. I returned the money writing: 'You know I won't leave this country.'

To have taken my father's money would have meant for me at the time a betrayal of my purpose in coming to Palestine. I think I would still feel that way today although one is supposed to mellow with age. My attitude, I am sure, is open to accusations of rigidity and my friends have often reproached me with this fault in my personality. But when I left Poland I believed something I continued to believe, which is that everything we had in Palestine should be created from the beginning. I knew how fundamental was our historical claim to the land. But I also knew that if we were to call it truly ours again, it must be earned with our toil. So living on handouts from my father, no matter how welcome, would not have suited my mission here.

Fortunately, with Spring, the malaria became less acute. Perhaps it was a psychological victory, mind over matter as it were, sparked by the doctor's ultimatum of go home or die. Probably it was a mere physiological immunization. In any case, one day I walked to the higher area of Rishon-Le-Zion where the colony was celebrating its twenty-fifth year. I had a temperature of 102 but I wanted to be present at this tribute to one of the first modern Jewish settlements. We drank wine and danced through the night and suddenly, I felt well. The attacks didn't come back so strongly after that. A few months later, when I moved up to the hills of Galilee with a group of young people, they disappeared almost totally.

When I arrived in Eretz Israel, I determined to speak only Hebrew. Unfortunately, this was impossible since the majority of immigrants spoke the various languages of exile: Yiddish, Ladino and practically all the tongues of Europe. I belonged to the Poalei Zion (Workers of Zion) political party and militated at its meetings for the adoption of Hebrew as the party's official language. Shortly before I left for the Galilee, I was asked to speak at a meeting of new arrivals from Europe. I got up and started to welcome them in Hebrew. I noticed the look of incomprehension on their faces. In a few minutes, people began to file out of the room. Rather than compromise with my belief, I continued in Hebrew. When I finished only three or four listeners were left before me. One of them turned out to be Itzhak Ben Zvi, who was to become Israel's second President. At that moment began my lifelong friendship and political association with this tall, deceptively fragile-looking man of sad and scholarly demeanour. His looks masked an abiding toughness. Though only in his twenties, Ben Zvi at the time we met was already a veteran of combat. He had been instrumental in organizing Jewish self-defence units in Russia against the wave of anti-Semitic pogroms there.

Both Ben Zvi and myself soon decided to leave the coastal plain for Galilee where the land was all but uninhabited and where we could settle it according to our ideal with others who spoke Hebrew or were willing to learn it and who belonged to our own generation.

In lower Galilee, we joined a group of pioneer labourers. Zemach was no longer with me. He had gone north some time before and was installed elsewhere. We still corresponded and though we differed in our political positions there was a lifelong bond between us. He died only a few years ago, in his eighties.

With my health restored, with a congenial group of like-minded people of my own age, and with real farming to do at last, I began to feel that now I was living the life I had always dreamt about.

I became a ploughman, working with two oxen. Though the work was hard, with food and living conditions very spartan, I enjoyed every minute of it.

My group was engaged in what we called 'the conquest of labour'. We would go out as a collective and work on land which the Jews themselves had bought and paid for through the Jewish National Fund or the Jewish Colonization Association. We would prepare a large patch of ground, make it ready for planting so that it could be settled rapidly by permanent settlers following on behind us. Then we would move off to work a new tract, perhaps a valley swamp or a boulder-strewn hillside. The idea was that we, who prepared the ground, would be permanent pioneers, moving from place to place on reclamation tasks, making the land fit for Jewish farm settlers. We had no thought at the time of becoming settlers ourselves. Ours was the job of creating farming opportunities for many other Jews who thus would not be at the mercy of reluctant employers. The pioneers I joined had their head-quarters in the settlement of Sejera and were the first 'conquest of labour' collective to engage in the task of reclamation.

In 1909, a similar outfit working in the Jordan valley decided to continue permanent settlement on a tract they themselves had prepared, and to continue living the collective life there. So was born kibbutz Degeniah, the first example of this unique form of social and economic organization where everyone in the community is an equal no matter what his or her task and where all share title both to the land and whatever its yield.

But describing it in this fashion makes the story of Degeniah over-simple. There were violent internal discussions within the pioneer group before it came to the decision to settle down. Yosef Bussel, the leading founder-member, had suggested that the pioneers stay and develop a particular site, which had

been little more than a malarial swamp. He said they should
not move on because developing the area on a permanent
basis was also a 'conquest of labour'. Some of his comrades
were horrified. Would not becoming permanent settlers
mean being 'owner-farmers', a hated class associated in their
minds with materialism and exploitation? To settle was not
'pioneering', they contended. Bussel told them this was non-
sense. They were not turning themselves into plantation
owners, hiring cheap Arab labour and sitting back to reap the
profits. They were proposing to continue as a collective, the
same as before. Everyone would go on working as he or she
had done, and the land would be owned by no one individually
but by all. The majority backed Bussel's idea and that is how
the first communal village, which in Hebrew is 'kibbutz',
began.

I do not think the pioneers of Degeniah were themselves
aware that what they were creating was unique, that others
would follow their pattern and their example, and that the
kibbutz idea would expand into a force of prime importance
in the country. Today, many of our best people are kibbutzniks. From this group come the majority of our officers, who
are picked on the basis of performance and for their leadership
potential. Although in the nation, the kibbutzim constitute a
minor element, their contribution to the economy is enormous, out of all proportion to their size. They are the key to
Israel's agricultural productivity. Then, too, the kibbutz has
evolved important provocative social practices such as having
children raised together but nevertheless in close contact with
their individual parents, who unlike parents elsewhere devote
two to three hours each afternoon to doing nothing but being
actively, completely with their children. One can say without
exaggeration that the kibbutzim constitute a social exper-
iment from which peoples everywhere can take inspiration
and ideas. And they are the one true example in today's
world of a democratic form of socialism, combining the most
advanced economic practices with a respect for individuality

and the inalienable rights of every human being, that has never been attained elsewhere.

No one could have foreseen that this influence on Jewish and universal values would grow from the modest settlement of Degeniah on the banks of the Jordan. Only much later did we come to recognize the greatness of the blessing hidden in the seed. Perhaps even now we are witnessing a mere fraction of the ultimate yield. For the sake of us all, I hope so.

My group stayed working in Sejera and the surrounding area for two years. Though most of us were new to manual labour, the labour itself caused little hardship. What hurt us more was worry and lack of sleep. At night, we had to guard against marauding Arabs and the threat of attack. We were an isolated community surrounded by nomadic Bedouins. Their intent was not to hurt us or to drive us away, but plain theft. They bothered the Arab settlements as much as they did us. The villages used to hire Circassian guards to keep watch over life and property. We in Sejera, true to the idea of being dependent on no one but ourselves, resolved to organize our own defence. To do otherwise seemed an abdication of our autonomy, the potential sacrifice of freedom.

Jews did not readily take to bearing arms. As a people we have an ingrained abhorrence to violence. In the centuries of exile we were often martyred. Yet we submitted in abnegation, rarely fighting back. Our weapons were intellectual, based upon reason and persuasion. Our brains were finely attuned to dialectical argument through long study of the myriad complexities in the Talmud, that great edifice erected during our dispersion to comment and elucidate the far greater edifice of the Bible. To take up arms seemed abnormal. It was all very well to buy land with the contributions of the mass of Jewry in the Diaspora. To cultivate that land in accordance with the pioneering ideal seemed the best way of spending one's life. But for Jews to take rifles and defend that which they had sown seemed at first as going too far.

But we knew that here in the Galilee – and the principle

holds true for Israel today if she is to survive, and she will – we knew there was no normality in the accepted sense of the term. We wanted to create a new life consonant with our oldest traditions as a people. This was our struggle. And to achieve that goal, we had to re-create everything from the beginning, to re-invent society. So we were prepared for blood on our hands in the name of autonomy, self-determination and self-defence.

Of course, we would fight only if attacked. But in that wild part of the country attack was inevitable. There was complete anarchy up there in the Galilee. A running battle was going on between various Arab bands, and between nomads and village folk. Defence of the settlements certainly didn't depend on the Turkish government since it had to all intents abandoned the country to its own devices. The only interest Turkey had in Palestine was the collecting of taxes, and even that its representatives didn't carry out efficiently.

The Circassians were good village guards but, for the reasons stated, we evolved our own defence organization called Hashomer, or 'The Watchmen'.

The story of how a band of apprentice farmers with a handful of ancient firearms gradually grew through many adventures and despite all manner of setbacks and vicissitudes into the Army of Israel is fascinating in its own right and I shall touch on it in another chapter. Suffice it to say here that being responsible for our own safety, we had to maintain constant vigilance, whatever our scruples about our weapons or, perhaps more significantly, our lack of skill with them. All of us laboured during the day as our tasks demanded the presence of every available hand. But at night, each took his round at guard duty. For a long time, nothing much happened. Occasionally a guard, sensing trouble, or letting his imagination get the better of him, fired a few shots into the darkness. So long as the Bedouins knew we were vigilant they kept their distance.

But one day, three of our group who were hiking back from

a short trip to the coast were ambushed by Arab nomads. A few wild shots were exchanged, both sides probably intending merely to scare the other. But an Arab bullet hit one of the Jewish boys and the incident turned into a pitched battle that ended with one Arab lying on the ground seriously injured. Our boys made it back to Sejera without further trouble and we were able to treat the wounded one who wasn't hurt seriously. But we knew that if the Arab bandit died, we could expect a vendetta of revenge that would unite nomads and villagers against us in accordance with the age-old law of an eye for an eye. Only in the Galilee, the practice was two eyes for one and vengeance would go on for a week, in an attempt to destroy everything we had created.

Well, the wounded man did die. We knew it when our sheep disappeared, stolen. Then, armed horsemen began roving menacingly round our settlement centre and our fields. All we could do was triple the guard and wait in anguish for an attack to come.

The first victim of this sorry situation was a newcomer, Israel Korngold. He had just joined the group and was taking one of his first turns at guard duty. He left the Sejera inn, our headquarters, at two in the afternoon armed with his rifle. Shots rang out. We grabbed our weapons and ran to help him. It was too late. He was lying dead on the road and his rifle was missing. That same day the Arabs killed a Jewish carpenter named Shimon Melamed. It was then I realized the wider implications of this small clash. Sooner or later, Jews and Arabs would fight over this land, a tragedy since intelligence and good will could have avoided all bloodshed. But all the intelligence and all the good will in the world would come to naught, I knew, faced with the rigid traditions and blood code of the East.

With all the danger, the tension at night and the hard work, I nevertheless was happy. I look on those days as perhaps the best of my life, when I felt everything I was doing had a purpose in the cause of building our new country. I was never so happy again or so at peace with myself until I came to the Negev only fifteen years ago, to work once more as a pioneer and to live again in the atmosphere of comradeship that I think is the essence of the pioneering spirit.

It was, therefore, a hard and painful decision for me to leave the Galilee for Jerusalem where some of my political friends were pleading with me to help run a monthly journal published by the Labour Zionist Movement. I had been active in discussions and conferences of the movement and had begun sending in articles to the journal, which was appearing erratically. When the organization decided to create a regular monthly, it asked Ben Zvi and me to take over. I declined at first as I had thrown myself fully into the pioneering life and hated the idea of leaving the open air, and the close friendships of the Galilee, for a desk job with all its petty irritations. But as I wandered round in my free hours to visit other pioneer outfits and met fellow workers from different parts of the country at occasional meetings and get-togethers, I became convinced that our efforts were seriously lacking in cohesion. We would never enlarge the opportunities for Jewish labour or secure dignified conditions of work for newcomers to the territory unless we were properly organized. Only when we had accomplished that first step and could insist that workers' standards be raised would we be in a position to seek the support of the Jewish community as a whole, a necessary pre-condition for dealing with the Turkish authorities on land matters and for securing appropriate rights for all our people in Palestine.

In 1910, therefore, I somewhat reluctantly agreed to become a journalist. Perhaps one of the minor points influencing my decision was that the nub of Zionist activity in the country had moved from Jaffa to Jerusalem, in symbolic emphasis of our affinity with the city which had always been and was to become once more our capital. I presented myself to the Labour Zionist Party's new headquarters there and went to work writing editorials for *Ahdout* (Unity), its Hebrew periodical.

At this time, I evolved a pen-name, a Hebraicized version of my own name, that I have used ever since. Hebraicizing one's name seemed to my generation a way of underlining our feeling for the country and our affinity with our ancestors. We were, in effect, indicating our purpose of taking up where they had left off. So David Gryn became David Ben-Gurion, in homage to a Jewish hero called Ben-Gurion who died defending Jerusalem against the final siege of the Roman legions in 70 C.E. That was the year from which our exile dates. The Romans over-ran the city after a siege that had cut its defenders off for thirty-six months. Jerusalem was put to the torch and the great Temple that Ezra had rebuilt disappeared in the flames, except for its famous Western Wall which became known to the Jews in dispersion as the 'wailing wall'.

In Jerusalem I led a busy life. We soon turned *Ahdout* into a weekly. I also helped in the organizational activities of the party, which was working to achieve three ends: to create a workers' syndicate, to unify Palestine's Jewish population and, as a further goal, to secure Jewish autonomy from the Ottoman administration.

Not a few times I regretted leaving the land. The fight for everything we wanted was uphill all the way. Even persuading our membership to consider Hebrew as the official language ran into resistance. A sizeable segment of the worker's movement wanted Palestine's Jews to speak the Yiddish mother-tongue of the majority, or German as a 'civilized' international vehicle of communication. Jerusalem itself, now one of the most striking cities in the world architecturally, was a miserable place in those days, physically more uncomfortable than Jaffa. It was a sprawling slum inhabited by the poor of every nationality, a true Tower of Babel. Winters were hard with driving rains and icy winds sweeping viciously across the hills, whistling down tortuous cobbled streets that never stayed on one level but meandered endlessly across the slopes on which the city perched precariously. Sometimes I doubted the effectiveness of what we were trying to do. The writing, meetings, discussions, conferences, plans and projects, that never seemed to end but never seemed to advance, would depress me. Journalism, like the never-ending lobbying that the well-dressed Zionists of Western Europe practised in the ante-rooms of Ministries, seemed to me futile compared to draining the swamps of the Galilee.

I realized, however, that someone with a healthy contempt for words without deeds, political castles-in-the-air, and sectarian intrigue, someone with a pioneering background had to represent the true builders of Eretz Israel. I am sure I would have continued to enjoy and to be very happy with the simple though hard life of a farm labourer. I certainly was glad to return to that life after more than half a century in politics. Yet I felt it my task to represent the ideal of active Zionism in Palestine at the organizational level where there was a vast educational and political programme to accomplish if we were ever to succeed in creating a force that would truly represent the Jewish ideal to the world from the vantage point of the pioneer on the spot in Palestine.

Looking back over my long life, I am glad that it took the turn it did. I am grateful to have been of service to a cause which I made my own from the very beginning of my days and which I have seen grow to fruition. I am also grateful for the wide-ranging and deeply satisfying existence it has been given me to enjoy.

4·Humanists and Fighters

David Ben-Gurion was instrumental in helping to organize Hashomer, the pioneers' rudimentary defence force. Later, under the British Mandate, he led the initiative, as head of the Palestine Histadruth or 'Federation of Jewish Labour', to develop Hashomer into a country-wide clandestine army. This was called Haganah, 'Defence'. Haganah's mission was to protect the Jewish communities from ever increasing Arab hostility as nurtured by Hadj Amin el Husseini, the fanatic Mufti of Jerusalem who dreamt of restoring a Moslem Caliphate over the entire Middle East. At the outbreak of the Second World War, Haganah furnished the majority of thirty thousand volunteer men and women from Palestine who fought under the British in the war against Nazism. Then, in the latter days of the Mandate, it struggled against the British immigration ban by organizing secret transport into the country. Ultimately Haganah became the backbone of the Israel Defence Forces.

Today, those who have passed through the military experience exhibit a spirit and outlook all their own. They can be described as uniquely Israeli. The young people from the Forces differ in their attitudes from older settlers or citizens. They represent a definite break with the Jewish past of Dispersion and a curious affinity with the nation of Biblical times. Along with the kibbutzim, with which it works in close collaboration, the military has set a tone. The issue of both, whether born in the country or recently arrived from elsewhere, has endowed this new nation with an indigenous personality.

As in earlier days, Ben-Gurion throughout his career in govern-

ment devoted much of his energy and thought to the country's military affairs. No one is better qualified to discuss the Israel Defence Forces as a national institution and the remarkable role they have played in moulding the younger generation into a cohesive entity.

A FOREIGN visitor once told me the story circulating in his country, which I trust is apocryphal, of two Israeli Cabinet Ministers discussing the national budget. One says: 'We must declare war on the United States!' The other looks at him in surprise. 'Yes,' explains the first, 'after we lose, the Americans will spend thousands of millions to rehabilitate us just as they did Germany and Japan.' The second Minister shakes his head sadly and asks: 'What if we win?'

This is a not very serious appreciation of our armed forces' phenomenal success in dealing with the enemy. But in oblique fashion, it does make the point that Israel's independence and its continuing survival are bound up with the history of our most successful national institution to date: The Israel Defence Forces (IDF). Reviewing my own contribution, I like to believe that I played a role in shaping this particular and in many ways unique expression of our Israeli personality.

Because everything touching military affairs occupied much of my energies for so long a period, I would like to discuss in some detail the thinking behind the IDF and all it stands for.

We abhor war and military things as ends in themselves. Nevertheless, the IDF is a source of deep national pride. Our armed forces have played a magnificent part in welding this diverse people into an entity in the course of only a few years. Were we able to throw down our weapons – and how gladly we should do so – to live in peace with our neighbours, we would still continue to depend on the dynamic represented today by the IDF to fulfil a vast assignment of national development. Not with bullets but with bulldozers and the other constructive tools of modern civilization.

In other words, national service has been a blessing for Israel. That this national service has of necessity concerned itself with military ends constitutes waste, tragic waste. We are well aware of that. But it has been the price of our survival.

Every thinking person in this country regrets the unhappy paradox that the most positive creation of a Jewish State should be an instrument of destruction. I have already remarked on how fundamentally alien to the Judaic character is violence, the abandonment of reason to mindless force. Having to bear arms is an affront to our Bible whereby we became the first people on earth to evolve formal concepts of personal liberty, of loving one's neighbour, of the sinfulness of killing and the moral desirability of beating swords into ploughshares, as our great prophet Isaiah enjoined us to do. It is also an affront to the concept of our basic right here in modern times as emanating from laborious cultivation of a barren, empty and neglected land. We take no joy, therefore, in the necessity of a huge, onerously expensive commitment to military defence.

Yet neither in our own nor in Biblical times have we been free of this commitment. Both we and our ancestors have had to assume the dual role of humanists and fighters. That our forebears knew how to defend themselves with fierce passion and efficiency is proved by their last stand against the Romans which, in all, endured from 66 to 73 in the Common Era. Seven years of resistance against the entire Roman Army! The siege of Jerusalem alone took three years and during that time no food reached the city. I consider it significant that even today, and despite the triumph celebrated in Rome after Jerusalem's fall, it is still considered bad luck to walk under the commemorative Arch of Titus erected by the Emperor Domitian in honour of the event and which stands in the Roman Forum.

The Roman conquest ended on a high plateau of the Negev

in 73 C.E. with the fall of Masada, the ancient fortress town of King Herod which we have now excavated and restored. All the citizens, men, women, children, preferred to die by their own hand rather than become Roman slaves. Masada was the Jewish equivalent to the Greeks' Thermopylae.

A look at the map indicates why there has always been conflict here. This relatively small country constitutes a permanent crossroads of three continents. Thus it is subject to the strains and pulls of world politics. In our time, oil, Soviet ambitions in the Middle East, the interests of the United States, Britain and France are far more responsible for maintaining the tension than the largely bogus pretext of Arab nationalism. If the Great Powers genuinely wanted peace, there would be no Arab–Israel conflict.

The revealing about-face undergone by Soviet policy *vis-à-vis* Israel is a good illustration in point. Up to 1954, the Russians had been our most fervent supporters. As soon as the British pulled out of Egypt, however, it became expedient for them to woo the Arabs and they began denouncing the very existence of the nation they were first in the world to recognize.

So the Soviets undertook their love affair with Egypt and systematically ruined that country's economy by selling it obsolete military equipment which it could ill afford to pay for. Who needs such friends?

How much more profitable for Egypt, and indeed all the Arab world, to realize that common interest lies in making peace and working together with us to create in the Middle East the world's richest garden – which it could easily become! The Egyptians can thank the Soviets, acting as tempters to military adventurism, for their war dead, the destruction or seizure of two entire military machines' worth of equipment, for bankruptcy both economic and political, for the closure of the Suez Canal and the loss of the Sinai Peninsula. We are most grateful that the Russian bear sees fit to hug our enemies to its imperious bosom. We shall continue to capture the weapons provided for our destruction and hurl them back at the enemy. We should, however, be even more grateful if the Arab world would finally see that only by standing with Israel in friendship and good will can the Middle East aspire to an independence and economic self-sufficiency never achieved in all its history but never so potentially achievable as now. The tragedy of the present conflict is ultimately this lack of fulfilment for the area as a whole, as well as for all the nations in it.

Our desire for peace is constant and we have proved its sincerity time after time. We are prepared to envisage important concessions in the name of a true negotiation with the nations that surround us. Certainly we stand ready to mobilize all the energy and skills we have been forced to develop and invest in defence, for the far more fruitful purpose of materially aiding our neighbours to attain levels of peaceful development compatible with the twentieth century. Our developmental goals are parallel to those professed by Nasser. How unfortunate for all concerned that for reasons of personal ambition and of facility, taking the course of least effort, he and his allies choose to remain blind to this.

That we have striven for peace while confronted by war is no mere phrase. Israel has always searched for rational, humane answers to its problem of survival even when there appeared small hope of finding them. Before independence, for instance, secret negotiations with King Abdullah of Transjordan were going on up to the very minute the Arab Legion marched at his order on Jerusalem. Hours before this event, the present Prime Minister, Mrs Golda Meir, went as my special envoy into Transjordan. At considerable personal risk, she crossed the frontier in Bedouin disguise and reached the King to plead for peace. To no avail!

Again, before the Sinai campaign of 1956, there were literally dozens of attempts to negotiate with President Nasser of Egypt or at least engage a dialogue. All manner of intermediaries were used in vain efforts to accomplish an Israel–Egypt meeting. Meanwhile, I did my utmost to secure formal guarantees from the world powers for the integrity of our frontiers and the free passage of shipping bound for our shores. Over and over again, I reiterated my readiness to leave immediately for Cairo, if need be, to sit down with Colonel Nasser face to face. All this to head off a conflict that we were confident of winning, that in the end we did have to fight and win.

Israel has indeed remained true to the ideas of peace and love of mankind on which the Bible rests. However, it is one thing to love your neighbour and another to commit national suicide.

That we are determined to remain here is self-evident. But it is worth examining some aspects of that determination. The Soviets have dared call us 'colonialists'. Their own savage oppression of Eastern Europe makes them self-styled experts in such matters, no doubt. Nevertheless, one can state categorically that no people in history arc less colonialist than we. Our claim to Israel is based on sweat, on digging the soil with our own hands, fertilizing, planting, harvesting, building, developing this beloved land of ours. We are known to fight with passion to defend it. Well, we have put everything we possess into it. That is the secret of our strength. And were we colonialists we wouldn't, we couldn't, have such strength!

It is again possible to say categorically that not by a single bullet or act of violence have Israel or the Jewish people in the twentieth century enforced their claim to this land. They have not affirmed their right to be here with arms, merely their right to remain. We have resorted to force in defence only. Despite the territorial gains our victories have achieved, our title here remains that which our toil has wrought. A comparison between the empty, stagnant, malaria-ridden Palestine of seventy years ago and the busy, up-to-date, ever developing Israel of today, gives the measure. And what we have today is of our own making entirely. Colonialism, the exploitation of one people by another, just doesn't enter into it.

The local Arab population, by the way, has been the first to profit from our development. The Arabs, like ourselves, no longer die of malaria, no longer live out their days in near starvation, unemployment, hopelessness. More and more, they are integrating themselves into the Israeli population, what with their representation in Parliament, the enrolment of their young into our system of compulsory education, the emancipation of their womenfolk and their presence as volunteers in the military. It is a subject I shall touch on elsewhere, but I do want to say here that our relations with the Arab minority is one of mutual respect on the human plane and of education towards attainment of twentieth-century levels on the plane of social institutions.

As early as 1917, the Balfour Declaration acknowledged internationally Israel's right to exist. Our remarkable progress in cultivating this land even then had made our claim obvious to the world. Recognition of our right to be here was confirmed several times during the years and finally by the United Nations' demand of Britain in 1947 that active steps be taken to establish a Jewish State in Palestine. All of which doesn't deny the right of any other people to have a State. Far be it from us to do such a thing. We were resigned in 1947 to receiving the rump end of Palestine in accordance with the United Nation's settlement. We didn't think that settlement very fair since we knew that our work here deserved a greater assignment of land. We didn't, however, press the point and prepared to abide scrupulously to international ruling come the day of our independence. We were also ready to see Jerusalem as an international city provided that the guarantees given by the United Nations to the Jewish population of its permanent right to live peacefully there and to participate in the city's democratic administration were respected. We had, therefore, absolutely no designs on Arab assigned areas.

But what happened? Our Jerusalem population was attacked even before independence. Our neighbours declared themselves our enemies and invited us to plunge into the sea, to abandon even that bit of land the whole world recognized as our own. And they set out to conquer us.

We Jews of Palestine had just watched in agony and helplessness as our brothers in the European lands, where many of us had originated, lined up in confusion and terror, divested of all belongings, even the clothes off their backs, for the journey into the gas chambers and ovens and starvation hells of the 'Final Solution'. We had witnessed this terrible abdication of humanity and we had all been marked by it.

If for no other reason than that of keeping faith with those who had died, we knew we must not walk in docility to the charnel house. So long as Israel lived, it would provide refuge from such atrocity. In the name of our persecuted dead we had to fight. If need be, we too would die. But in the manner of the Jewish heroes in the Warsaw ghetto, in Jerusalem besieged by the Romans, at Masada: backs to the wall, giving the enemy no quarter.

We were not, I hasten to point out, interested in dying or becoming martyrs. No more are we today. The Jews have had quite enough of that in their long history. We were and are concerned with life, with making Israel flourish, with showing mankind as a whole how one can create a land of plenty from a patch of wilderness. We came here in joy and hope, in devotion to our people, our heritage, our age-old vocation of contributing to humanity's well-being. Wherever there have been Jews, culture has flourished, humanity has advanced. We wished, and still do, to contribute our presence to the Middle East as a whole. I know that someday we shall be allowed to do so.

I think these preliminary comments, mostly on the subject of peace, provide a necessary background to the story of our Defence Forces, their role today as well as their official birth in the midst of conflict as Israel struggled for independence. Keeping in mind our fundamental abhorrence of everything touching war and violence, and our belief in the Middle East's capacity for peaceful union, one can grasp the uniqueness of the IDF as an institution.

There is one comment more that must be made at this juncture. In recent times Israel has had to contend with charges of aggression. Since it is my deepest conviction that we are not now nor ever will be an aggressor nation, I wish to answer these charges.

Aggressiveness is another term used by the Soviet Union and its satellites to characterize our efforts at self-defence. It is perhaps easy for a nation possessing one sixth of the earth's total land mass within its borders to criticize the swiftness that so tiny a nation as Israel must deploy in meeting any threat to its frontiers. We shall not linger on the jumpiness the Russians themselves recently exhibited, big as they are, in their dispute with the Chinese over a mud flat neither have found use for since the two nations began. Israel can answer the epithets tossed at it by the self-evident observation that our geography demands we apply the rule: he who strikes first wins the battle. Otherwise, we should be overwhelmed. We have never hidden our intention of pursuing this tactic and indeed have warned our Arab enemies time and again that parading armoured columns along our borders, firing on our farmers, ploughing their fields, invading our airspace, stepping up terrorist raids on our territory, would have to be met with hard-hitting action on our part.

Let us take the best example of all: June 1967. Before the Six Day War, Nasser was literally brandishing his heavy tanks, courtesy of the USSR, at us on the Gaza strip frontier. The Gaza region faces our most populous, built-up and flattest area, Israel's single most vulnerable territory. Meanwhile, the Syrians fired on our kibbutzim from the Golan Heights, killing Israeli civilians day after day, and invaded our airspace with their MIG fighter planes. Then Nasser prevailed upon the United Nations to withdraw its troops from the Tiran Straits which he took over, announcing loudly that henceforth the port of Eilath was cut off to world shipping.

At that point, we had one of two choices. We could wait in passive apprehension, as the world exhorted us to do and rather in the manner of the European countries before the Second World War, for the the Arab 'Anschluss', as it were. Or we could take preventive action. Waiting meant sitting by until Tel Aviv, Jerusalem, Haifa, our painfully cultivated lands and our factories went up in smoke under the impact of the enemy's Soviet bombers. It meant potentially sacrificing thousands of Israeli lives. With less than three million people in our total population, we could not lightly contemplate such a loss. Especially not after what had happened to the Jews of Europe.

In any event, waiting would have meant sacrificing all military advantage and the consequent endangering of Israel's very existence.

What did we do, therefore? Well, first we went to the United Nations. Secondly, we published warning after warning to the Arab nations and to President Nasser in particular that we could not allow ourselves to be subject to such pressurings. We clearly outlined our intentions and pleaded to be left in peace. The answer: stepped up Arab hysteria and anti-Jewish propaganda. Our reluctance to fight was taken for weakness, instead of the attempt at reasonableness that it was. Nasser and his friends began to anticipate quick victory, a lift to Arab unity that might make the restive populations of those countries forget for a little while their material backwardness and the indifference of their governments to their misery.

After the closing of the Tiran Straits and the UN's hasty departure – over which I shall pass in silence as words fail in face of this unilateral and somewhat less than adroit initiative – there was nothing for it. We struck. Our first objective was the saving of Israeli lives by knocking out enemy aircraft before they could get into the air and hurt us. In the final analysis we had to attack or die. So much for our 'aggressiveness' in the Six Day War.

It is the same with our retaliation for the recurring attacks perpetrated by the Arab powers on our country today. We take no pleasure in punitive raids and other measures taken to curb enemy violations of the present ceasefire agreements. But survival dictates that so small a nation as Israel must do its utmost to discourage continual attack from its far more populous neighbours.

Let me add that even with defence so major a preoccupation, the mission of our armed forces remains as oriented towards constructive ends such as education and the unifying of Israeli youth through common training and experiences as it does towards warfare. There could be no greater antithesis than the IDF to a war machine of the classical type, nor to an instrument of fanaticism and conquest on the order of Hitler's goose-stepping storm troopers.

5·Independence

On the Sabbath eve of 14 May 1948, the fifth day of Iyar 5708, David Ben-Gurion stood before a hastily convened Provisional Government in Tel Aviv and read out a formal Proclamation of Independence that in the Land of Israel was established a Jewish State – the State of Israel.

Dawn the next morning saw Egyptian bombers over the city. The infant nation was in a life-and-death struggle against seven better equipped, numerically superior, British trained – and in some cases led – Arab armies invading its meagre territory from every side. With inadequate weapons, farm implements, their bare hands and indomitable spirit, the Israelis sent the enemy reeling. The Arab military commanders had scheduled the conquest of Tel Aviv for 25 May. By 10 June, however, they were glad to accept truce. Later, further Arab aggression resulted in consolidated and enlarged frontiers for Israel. Finally, by terms of an armistice signed with the Arab powers in 1949, Israel knew peace.

OUR Defence Forces as they are today grew from the War of Independence and the many lessons, some of them indeed painful, learned at the time. That we were able to meet the Arab onslaught with any organized defence at all is something of a miracle, directly due to the existence of Haganah as developed from Hashomer in the early days of pioneering.

I should emphasize that, whereas the surrounding Arab countries were building modern armies under British tutelage, the conditions of the Mandate precluded most open military development on our part. Before the White Paper of 1939 severely restricting our activities, and in reaction to incessant Arab rioting provoked by the Jerusalem Mufti, the Mandatory Administration did let us train a 2,000 man Jewish Settlement Police. During the Second World War, before the formation of the Jewish Brigade which fought with the British Army in Europe, we were also allowed to organize Palmach, or 'The Striking Force', a commando unit that ultimately trained about 2,500 women and men. The British realized that if Palestine ever entered the war, they would need the support of a Jewish attack outfit highly trained in commando activities and not prone to wavering loyalties as Arab soldiers might be.

The post-war period began with a ruthless crackdown by the British Labour government on Jewish immigration and all Jewish defence initiatives. Haganah thereupon earned British enmity by devoting itself to illegal immigration. Its leadership went underground moving from kibbutz to kibbutz. Whenever the British caught suspected Haganah members they threw them in jail. They were forever confiscating our painfully gathered stores of arms and vehicles, many of these admittedly stolen from Mandate supply depots. But meanwhile the surrounding Arab countries continued to receive British weapons, artillery, armour, warplanes, the normal engines of war. British officers trained their armies and, in the case of Transjordan's Arab Legion, commanded them. So the situation was very one-sided and decidedly not in our favour.

The story, however, should really begin in the days of Hashomer for those times set the tone and cadence of our subsequent military development.

I did mention that among the Jews there were early doubts as to the justification of bearing arms in self-defence. In 1906 this was a controversial issue of the day. Such theoretical questions as when does defence become offence were debated at great length among the pioneers themselves, many of whom had a philosphical bent of mind.

Regretfully, the sight of our dead, killed by Arab marauders, cut theory short. The debate ended with the Watchmen taking up arms.

As it turned out, and here is a paradox indeed, Hashomer's existence smoothed the way for peaceful Jewish–Arab relations in the Galilee. The Moslem villagers had evidently been shocked at our failure to provide for our own defence. Among themselves, they had referred to us contemptuously as 'children of death', meaning that our diffidence to bearing arms was interpreted by them as evidence of cowardliness and a shameful love of death. From the time Hashomer came on the scene, and proved its efficiency in skirmishes with roving bandits, the Galilee Arabs viewed us with new respect. They acknowledged our equality with themselves and, what was and is of capital importance, our right to be their neighbours. Is it just coincidence that the Galilee has always been the calmest part of Israel where Arab–Jewish relations have taken their most peaceful and fruitful turn? I think not!

After the First World War when the Turks were driven out of Palestine and the British assumed control of the country, Hashomer was no longer sufficient to satisfy the defence needs of a growing and increasingly diverse Jewish community. The entire outfit of Watchmen numbered no more than forty men and women whose full time was thus employed.

We now needed a popular organization embracing the bulk of able-bodied Jews who would continue to work at their normal jobs but also be given regular military training and then put to organizing the security of their communities. I should add that many a kibbutz, settlement, village and out-post was isolated, exposed at all times to attack. There was great need of a defence system to link up these communities and Hashomer wasn't adequate to the task.

Thus we created Haganah as the defence arm of the

Histadruth, the General Federation of Jewish Labour in Palestine of which I was the first Secretary-General. Since Histadruth was the country's largest Jewish association, its sponsorship ensured the spreading of a military defence programme throughout our population. Most of Haganah's early members were Histadruth workers who considered it also their mission to support the socialist ideal. However, as problems of security loomed ever larger, Haganah became totally preoccupied with defence and political ideology was dropped.

Haganah was chronically poor in arms and equipment. But it was exceedingly well endowed with self-discipline. Throughout the 1920s and 1930s Jewish communities suffered all manner of harassment by Arab fanatics, mainly stirred to action through the machinations of Mufti el Husseini. Husseini, who spent the Second World War in Nazi Germany and ended up a wanted criminal, was directly responsible for provoking a series of Jewish massacres during the pre-war period. More than once Haganah was moved to consider an all out retaliation on Arab communities. It always restrained itself and confined its activities strictly to defence. The coolness and self-discipline of our armed defenders prevented the country from succumbing to the flames of civil war at this time.

I have already mentioned Haganah's contribution to the British war effort against Hitler and its subsequent struggle against the British ban on Jewish immigration. I should add that Haganah formed the nucleus from which were recruited those brave women and men who served behind enemy lines in Nazi-occupied Europe to lend what aid they could to the beleaguered Jewish population in these areas.

At the time independence became a certainty, our main problem was that of acquiring arms. One didn't have to be clairvoyant to know the Arabs would immediately attack us. Their attitude was more than plain. I am speaking now not of the Palestinian Arabs among whom nationalistic feeling was non-existent, but of the surrounding Arab nations who for a variety of political reasons had determined to play the anti-Jewish card. Transjordan, later Jordan, did in fact profit from the situation in 1948 by grabbing a goodly piece of land along the river Jordan's West Bank that it was supposed to be preserving for the much talked of but constantly ill-used Palestinians. Far from giving this land to its so-called 'blood brothers' of Palestine, Jordan stuffed the latter into concentration camps and kept the territory for itself. International contributions of food and money to aid these miserable refugees were then siphoned off by the governments supposedly defending their cause. All of this is hardly my affair. I merely want to indicate why I am indifferent to the outcries of the Arab nations concerning both the Palestinians' non-existent 'quest for independence' and their championship of it. Israel's disappearance tomorrow might produce a Jordanian, Syrian, Egyptian and Iraqi squabble over the spoils, another Middle East 'problem', as it were. I can guarantee that the one thing it wouldn't produce is true Palestinian independence. That is one reason the present situation is so utterly irresponsible, tragic in its meaninglessness. The ostensible cause for which the Arabs fight is no cause, other perhaps than hatred of one people for another. But if mankind is going to survive the atomic age this sort of hatred will have to cease. The Arab future as much as our own depends on overcoming it in the Middle East.

Having digressed so far, I must go on to say that in 1948 it was the Arab powers and not the Jews who exhorted the local Moslem population to leave their homes and their land. We asked them to stay and help us build a modern country. Those who left did so far more in fear of Arab threats of reprisal against 'disloyalty' than of their Jewish neighbours. In confidence they emigrated across the frontiers to the Arab nations which had demanded they come. They ended up in the foul conditions we know of.

Today, there is a new problem. A generation has grown up

in the squalor and bitterness of the refugee camp atmosphere. This generation covets Israel as a confined man covets freedom. Anything to escape from present conditions. Who can blame these young people? Certainly not I. They are a stunted, embittered, and I fear half-crazed handful of human beings existing on the margin of history and cut off from all roots due to the tragic error of their parents in trusting to false allies. Our hearts genuinely go out to them. But their plight is not of our making. By this statement I'm not trying to absolve us from a human responsibility to help them as best we can and if they will let us. But I am affirming that we just are not the cause of their homelessness and their misery. Israeli Arabs aren't miserable. They don't live in concentration camps. They are not exiles. In fact, they enjoy the highest standards of any Arab peoples' in the world today! They constitute those who stayed on and who, for the most part, gave their allegiance to Israel, the only democratic State this territory has known in thousands of years.

The fact that we are not responsible for the Palestine refugee problem does not mean we aren't concerned with it. We are willing to go far in helping to resolve it to the best of our limited means. We can only contribute to its resolution, however, if the other side recognizes the Frankenstein monster its ill-advised policies have created, and helps too.

Regarding the refugee camp offspring, sympathetic as we are to their condition and to its unfortunate causes, we cannot tolerate their criminal activities. One can deplore juvenile delinquency and publish analyses of its etiology; one cannot tolerate the delinquency itself. The case of Israel *vis-à-vis* the lunatic fringe issuing from these camps is the same. I think many an Arab government secretly agrees with our position. These people are now a source of danger for everyone. President Nasser and King Hussein of Jordan never know when some wild-eyed offspring of the camps will burst in on them, machine gun in hand. The latest trick of hijacking the world's civil airliners will hardly endear these unfortunates to humanity at large.

To return to our problems of 1947 and 1948. We had no illusions about being allowed to live in peace with the advent of independence. We had to prepare as best we could against the aggression we foresaw as a matter of course. Yet we could not arm, nor carry out military exercises except in strictest secret and under very limiting conditions. Our people had to face war almost without preliminary training.

Haganah did its best to keep abreast of the situation. On the kibbutzim, it furtively drilled farmers in rifle practice; it mounted secret workshops where old trucks were provided with light machine guns and somewhat pathetic metal shields, vulnerable as it turned out even to small arms' fire, attached to bumpers and sides. These vehicles we called 'armoured cars'. As such, they served heroically in one of the great exploits of Jewish history: the rescue of Jerusalem in April 1948.

As head of the Jewish Agency, the administrative body linking the Jewish community of Palestine with the Diaspora, I had for years (ever since the Biltmore Conference in 1941) been preoccupied with purchasing military equipment abroad. We had stockpiled some reserves here and there in the world. But what good could they do us waiting in some far off country? I am glad that I had sufficient grasp of our future needs to invest the limited funds at my disposal not only in weaponry but also in machine tool equipment for the production, autonomously within the country, of armaments and heavy military machinery such as amphibious bridge spans and the like. But again, we dared not bring this precious material in while the British and the threat of confiscation remained.

When we started the War of Independence, we had 45,000 able-bodied women and men connected with Haganah and Palmach. In addition, several thousand more people belonged to various 'private' armies that operated on their own. More of these later. Of the 45,000 available to the government, we could arm only about three-quarters. And we didn't have enough ammunition to supply even this reduced group effectively. For the rest, we had to rely on homemade devices such as Molotov cocktails and the like.

We did have an 'airforce' of sorts: a handful of light sports and training planes belonging to various aero clubs here and there. We hastily mounted machine guns aboard these craft. 'Bombing' consisted of lobbing grenades out of the cockpit!

On the feverish night when the British pulled out and we declared the State of Israel, we had no way of knowing what would happen. Could our people, ill-prepared as they were, rise to the occasion? I knew they had it in them to do so. I was confident in their fortitude. But materially we were so very badly off.

Yet we all took courage from the magnificent rescue of Jerusalem undertaken by Palmach a few days previously, in the first week of April 1948. The situation then was grim indeed. The Arabs had cut off the water supply to the modern Western sector of the city where the Jewish population predominated. As the Romans in 70 C.E., they planned to deprive the Jewish inhabitants of all sustenance and so force capitulation to *de facto* Arab rule. On 11 March they had blown up the Jewish Agency headquarters in the city and by mid-March were threatening the single two-lane highway from the Jewish coastal settlements, the lifeline which our population in Jerusalem depended on for food and vital necessities.

The crisis came on 30 March when the Mufti's men attacked a large convoy trying to get up to the city. It was a slaughter and dozens of our trucks were also destroyed. We realized that the road to Jerusalem was definitively cut. Colonel Lund, a Norwegian representative of the United Nations Mission in Palestine, summed up our strategic position when he said: 'Your situation is worse than that of Norway in 1940.' Encouraging words!

The British failed to intervene to protect our people or clear the road. In fact, on one occasion in March, they stopped a Jewish truck convoy, disarmed its members and subsequently distributed their weapons to the Arabs. So we knew it was up to us. Palmach, assembling what vehicles it could, fought its way mile by mile up that narrow, twisting road. It had constantly to battle the enemy from below, which meant being at a permanent tactical disadvantage. There were close combat engagements at every turn. Vehicle upon vehicle dropped by the wayside, prey to anti-tank weapons and grenades. They stand there today, rusted over and strange looking in the peaceful shrubbery beside the busy highway. They are a monument to those young commandos who fought and died for Jerusalem. Despite the losses of vehicles and lives, Palmach beat the Arabs back, made it to the city gates, re-established the links with the water reservoirs. It also got in three large convoys of supplies before being forced to relinquish the road. These enabled the citizens of West Jerusalem to hold out against the Arab Legion on near hunger rations until the siege was finally lifted in June.

Of course, in Jerusalem there was also the tragic loss of the Jewish Quarter in the Old City – the quarter holding our oldest shrines and monuments. The community there, mostly elderly people who had been joined by a small Haganah detachment, had few weapons, little ammunition, almost no food. It was surrounded by tens of thousands of Arabs and invaded by the Legion. It finally surrendered, the people retreating as best they could to the New City where those who survived joined the fighters there.

In that dark period following independence, I don't know of anyone in the Provisional Government who wasn't tortured by second thoughts. Were we justified in calling upon our people to resist if resistance meant mass slaughter? We knew, however, that it was once again a case of all or nothing. There was no alternative to fighting back.

Whether we could hold out was another question.

Hundreds of settlements throughout the country found themselves isolated and under enemy attack. In these places, people had only their own spirit and ingenuity to count on. Even the leadership couldn't guess at the heroism, steadfastness and determination to stand the ground this spirit would call up. Words cannot do justice to the acts of devotion, both individual and collective, carried out by our citizens in the name of their new State of Israel. If ever an enemy was turned back by the unflinching will of a people, it was here in 1948. This went for everyone, regardless of age or sex. The women, of course, fought alongside the men in every combat entity. Since there weren't enough adults to go around, support for the fighting troops came from the children and old people. Our teenagers who had received special training in Haganah's clandestine youth camps took over the vital job of communications. Israel's 'signal corps', a lifeline indeed, was manned by fourteen and fifteen-year-olds!

The example of kibbutz Yad Mordechai stands as a typical and noble act of Israeli resistance during the first round of the War of Independence. The kibbutz was right on the Gaza strip frontier and one of the first spots in the country to bear the full force of an Egyptian armoured infantry onslaught. How the Jews did it, I don't know. But day after day they beat back Egyptians, holding them off with rifles, home-made grenades, tractors, pitchforks, stones, anything they could lay their hands on. When the central buildings so lovingly erected out of many years' kibbutz profits were burnt to the ground, they retreated into the barns and fought the enemy there, step by step, wall by wall, ruin by ruin. Eventually, Yad Mordechai did collapse. But by its resistance the Kibbutzniks had dislocated the entire military timetable of the Egyptian Army. An operation scheduled to take an hour or so the mere rounding up by a mechanized army of a few civilians, had lasted six days with the Egyptians halted at Israel's very frontier! That was typical of the resistance the Arabs encountered everywhere. They had the steel, the manpower. We had only our total refusal to yield.

If isolation and lack of weaponry were the main difficulties that the population-at-large had to contend with, at headquarters, where I had assumed responsibility for military operations, we had a different order of problem.

Firstly, we had to adjust our thinking from the local, 'fire brigade' type of defensive actions we had always fought up to now to the prosecution of war at a national level and on several fronts. Before independence, no major military units, not even a full brigade, had ever been committed to battle. Only small groups of people had defended specific places or executed specialized actions such as Palmach's drive on Jerusalem.

Now it was imperative to order each action in accordance with a much vaster situation. We couldn't rush here and there defending villages and towns piecemeal. We daren't even waste our tiny reserves on rescuing Jerusalem's Old City, despite the popularity of such a course. I told the officers of the hastily named headquarters staff: 'We have to concentrate our forces and commit them in accordance with an overall plan to strike at the enemy armies. To destroy their fighting machine, we must go over to the counter-attack fighting them not only in the sectors of Israel which they have invaded but also in their territories. We must carry the battle over to them.'

This was easier said than done. We had first to resolve some serious administrative difficulties at home and within our own ranks.

Adjusting to nationhood, especially in the midst of war, is no easy task for the mind. In our newly created State, a few of the leaders themselves had difficulty in realizing that they were no longer nurturing a trade union movement, or a secret band of guerrilla fighters or even a political party, but indeed that their hands were on levers controlling the destiny of an entire country. Those of us who had made the adjustment, knew that the first long-term necessity was to bring in modern armaments, the heavier the better. But some of our colleagues objected at first to spending money on these major weapons. 'What do you want with tanks, guns and bombers?' I recall one Cabinet Minister asking at a time when the Egyptians were threatening the Galilee and had already cut off the Negev. And I remember another who was 'disturbed' at the idea that Israel should have a police force!

A State is a State, and especially so beleaguered a one as Israel required the organs of external and internal security with all their elaborate modern appurtenances whatever our ultimate ideals of peace and brotherhood. I am proud to say, however, that our national democracy never suffered from the pressure of events. Israel has always remained true to its founding principles of representative government, an independent judiciary (the true safeguard of any democracy), the guarantee of civil rights for all citizens, freedom of speech and of the press, freedom of worship and a fundamental belief in the dignity of the individual. In our darkest moments, no attempt was ever made to curb these liberties – and often enough the young government had to answer minority political dissent at home while fighting off the enemy.

Our military set up in 1948 also suffered from an amateurism that, although heroic, lacked discipline and cohesiveness. The hierarchy of command had to be affirmed if we were to hold out. And this was difficult to achieve for a fighting force that had always battled spontaneously and in tiny units.

Jews being the individualists they are, much of Haganah, the Palmach units and the several private armies that were waging war in their own way and under their own command, had little notion of the primordial necessity of obeying directives from a centralized source, namely our headquarters, that could keep the general picture in mind. 'Who are they to tell us what to do?' more than one battlefield commander would demand. There were many instances when we in Tel Aviv were disobeyed, the combat units affirming their right to run themselves. Palmach in particular took the view that it was self-sufficient and accountable only to its own chiefs. During the second truce of 1948, by which time we were stronger, the battle situation was better under control and we could even think of winning the war, I was obliged to disband Palmach on the imperative that it must integrate its effectives into the national Army.

That the military command had to be centralized was so important that I made use of an incident of the first truce in June 1948 to achieve this end. The private Irgun Zvi Leumi force, numbering about three thousand people, was the focal point of this initiative on which I staked the government's ability to lead the nation.

When the United Nations negotiated that first cessation of hostilities between ourselves and the Arab powers in June, both sides agreed not to rearm during the four week truce period. The injunction was far more serious for us than for our enemies since indirect combatant countries such as Saudi Arabia could stockpile armaments and send them into the belligerent countries when fighting resumed. We had no such possibility and were in desperate need of reinforcement. Yet, I knew that for us the promise was a test. Did we have the maturity to be a nation, to belong to the family of civilized nations? If the answer was yes, we had to prove it by resisting the temptation to break a promise we had made. At that time, it was important to retain the confidence of the United Nations by the straightforwardness of our conduct. I also knew that more significant than arms was the moulding of our forces into an entity that could function at a truly national level both strategically and in the deployment of force to carry out that strategy.

During the truce, we trained intensively with the weapons we had and frantically repaired all the smashed material we could possibly resuscitate. But we forebore to import even those arms already bought, paid for and en route to us before the truce.

Irgun violently disagreed with this policy. It was expecting an arms' shipment from Czechoslovakia aboard the freighter *SS Altalena*. It announced its intention of defying the government ban and landing these weapons clandestinely when the freighter arrived.

I decided this must be the moment of truth. Either the government's authority would prevail and we could then proceed to consolidate our military force or the whole concept of nationhood would fall apart. Once again, this idea had to be hammered home to the Jewish leadership. There wasn't time to debate the niceties, the fine points of the situation. I knew we would never succeed in holding off the Arab armies with amateur heroics no matter how admirable the individual acts of courage and sacrifice involved. A nation was at stake. Not a farmhouse, road or town, but a nation. So I made my stand.

When the *Altalena* arrived and, in defiance to clear government injunction, the arms were being smuggled onto a beach, I ordered the Army to fire on the ship. Jews were firing on Jews in the midst of a fight to the death with the entire Arab world! Would the Army obey or would there be chaos?

In the event, my orders were carried out. The unloading of those arms we needed so desperately was stopped. Irgun and all the fighting forces were made to realize that changing times demanded subordination to the national will as expressed by those whom the people would designate to govern and command militarily.

The incident caused near civil war among the Jews themselves. But in the eyes of the world we had affirmed ourselves as a nation. When the smoke cleared and the indignation died down, the population-at-large put itself squarely behind its government. The days of private armies were past and in the manner of every other well organized state, we had the makings of a central command under government control. With this achieved, we went on to provide the co-ordinated effort that in the course of a year brought us victory beyond our most hopeful expectations.

(*Above*) David Ben-Gurion (centre) with his fellow workers at the wine cellars of Rishon-le-Zion in 1907.

(*Below*) Tel Aviv's founders meet (1908) to draw lots for land on the sand dunes outside Jaffa.

David Ben-Gurion, a student of law in Turkey, 1914.

(*Above*) The editorial board of the *Poalei Zion* journal *Ha'ahdut* (The Unity), founded in 1910. Left to right: Itzhak Ben-Zvi, Ya'akov Zerubavel, David Ben-Gurion, and Rachel Yana'it.

(*Below*) David Ben-Gurion, a soldier in the Jewish Legion, 1918.

Workers at Nahalat, in the Jezreel Valley in 1922, beside the swamps they were fighting to drain.

(*Above right*) Jewish leaders in conference with Neville Chamberlain and other ministers at St. James's Palace, 1939. Ben-Gurion in the foreground, on the right of Chaim Weizmann.

(*Below right*) Ben-Gurion signs the Declaration of Independence, 1948. Seated beside him is his foreign minister, Moshe Sharett, later to become Prime Minister.

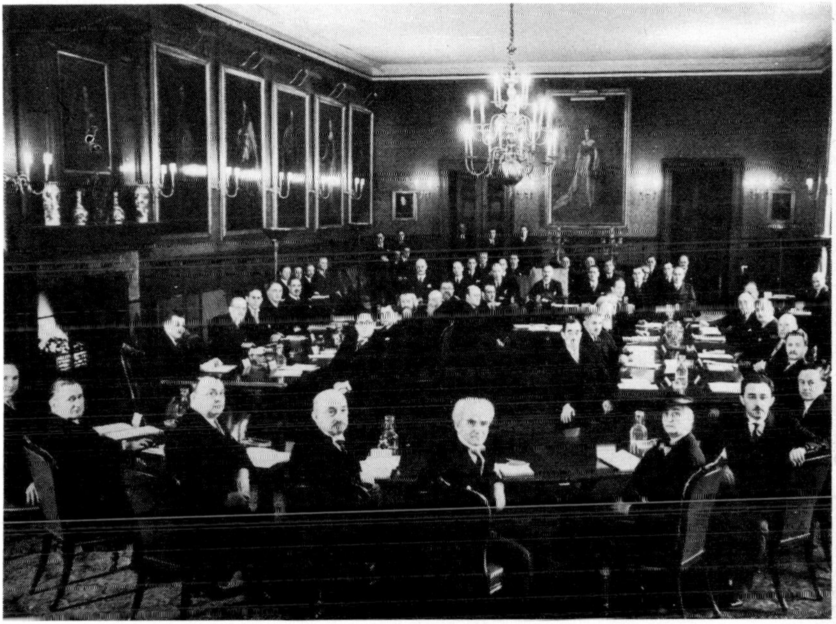

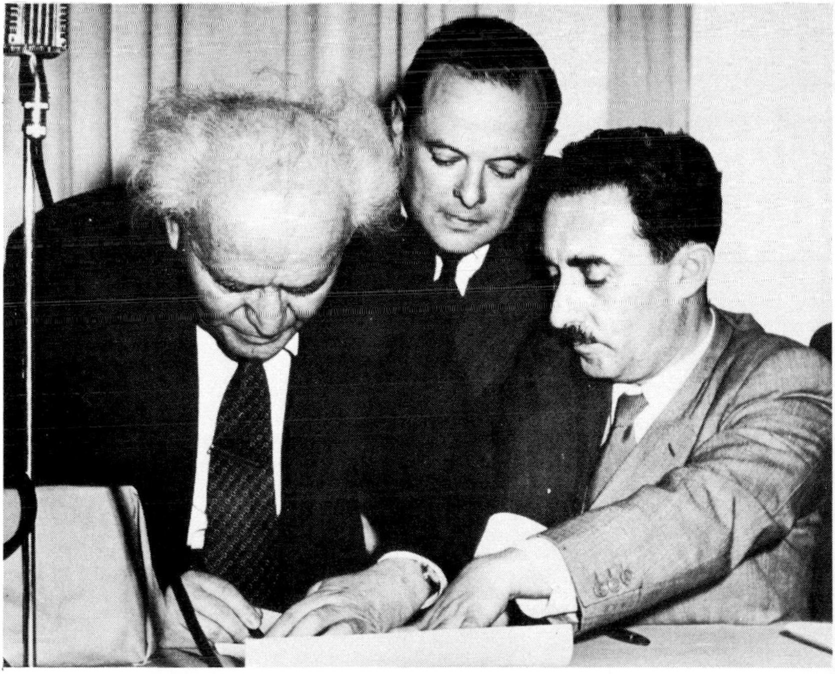

David Ben-Gurion at Kibbutz *Sde Boker*, in the Negev.
He retired to this outlying settlement after his resignation from
the government in 1953.

An Israeli commander briefs his officers for battle during the
Sinai Campaign of 1956.

David Ben-Gurion at the desert graveside of his wife Paula.

6·Democracy and the Military Today

The peace which in 1949 Israel found for the first time was a very uneasy one punctuated by raids of Egyptian fedayin commandos, economic embargo, the ever-present threat of an enemy at every frontier – and in some areas, Israel was then less than nine miles wide! Between 1949 and the Sinai campaign of 1956, no less than 1,250 Israelis died in local incidents and terrorist attacks. Many more were injured. Nevertheless, the country as a whole now had a breathing spell, a time to create national institutions, to consolidate energies and to build a modern defence force.

BECAUSE military preoccupations rank so high in national life, I am often asked whether there is danger that democracy will fail in Israel. I think it inconceivable. I shall endeavour to explain why.

I have tried to show how far we are from being militarist in attitude. We are also as far removed as one can imagine from the totalitarian outlook. Put two Jews together and you have a political argument. Put two Israelis together and you have opposing political parties. The contentiousness I discovered on my first setting foot in Jaffa has never diminished in Israeli political life. No people I can think of have less talent for submitting to dictatorship than the Jews, and in particular the Israelis.

A look at our defence system, the most disciplined organization we have in the country, indicates just how much we predicate our very existence on democracy and on the popular consent that only this form of government can elicit.

Judaism traditionally embraces the democratic concept of social conduct by stressing the individual's inward control of himself through the workings of personal conscience over outward forms of restriction. The individual's capacity to contribute to the group is considered voluntary and emanates from within himself. This is the dynamic at work in our Defence Forces today and, so I believe, accounts for their extraordinary spirit. It is in essence a democratic spirit, though it makes use of military discipline. The discipline is certainly there as it has to be, yet officers and men are on first name terms, they socialize off duty, they serve under similar conditions, wear the same uniform except for a small insignia, live largely the same lives. And if anyone attempted to impose upon them the classical, Prussian-type concepts of militarism such as 'to obey is to obey', or 'you are not here to think', or the European soldiers' maxim of 'never under any circumstances volunteer', they would laugh in such a person's face. Insubordination is no problem in Israel. But people obey not because of threats and Articles of War so much as out of respect for their commanders' ability to judge a situation. They know that he or she has been picked for qualities of military leadership only and trained specifically to lead. A good number of our officers are chosen on the record of battlefield performance.

I would say that not only do the Israel Defence Forces pose no threat to our internal freedom, but that they actively contribute towards maintaining its integrity. In this sense, as in day-to-day operations, our military establishment is like no other in the world.

Basically, our Army, Navy, Air Force – all of which operate under unified command, thus eliminating the classical inter-service rivalries so common elsewhere and so wasteful of effort – are a voluntary association of citizens profoundly oriented towards civilian life. They have dedicated themselves temporarily to national security in our country's great need. Of course, we have conscription and regulations regarding the national service of young people. But these measures were taken and are maintained by Parliamentary law and democratic common consent as they are in other countries. The high number of volunteers who enter the paratroops, our military youth groups and special corps – I shall describe one of these, Nahal, later – indicates the willingness with which our young men and women submit to national responsibility. The remarkable lack of disciplinary infractions and misdemeanours committed by service people also attests to a general good will.

In themselves, these indications are salutory but hardly unexpected. Every major community in Israel is within ten minutes, jet bomber time, of a hostile frontier. The general support of the military by the citizenry comes from personal awareness of the enemy's presence.

However, the civilian orientation of even our highest ranking officers is a truly special characteristic and one that I consider gives a dimension to our military organization few others possess.

When I speak of a civilian orientation I am certainly not talking about lack of military proficiency. Watch the Israel Army at drill or the Air Force and Navy at manoeuvres and you'll see a very high level of competence in the classical military arts. I challenge any European Army, including the most traditionalist, to better our standards!

I do mean, however, that our military is very far removed from career-oriented, caste-bound tradition. The IDF is not a club, a lifetime sinecure, a catch-all for people with nothing better to do than dress up in uniform. Foreign observers are always surprised at the youthfulness of our highest ranking officers. Traditionally (and after twenty years we do have traditions!), the Chief of Staff himself is in his forties and on temporary appointment only. This means even officers who are serving full time can expect to leave active duty early in life and pursue subsequent civilian careers. It also means we don't have, in the European tradition, a staff of conformists at the top perpetually fighting the last war. In our position, we could hardly afford that.

Our top military talent has repeatedly gone on to distinguish itself in the university, the law, politics, diplomacy, business, the pioneering life of the kibbutzim, technology and almost any other dynamic activity one could name. Often these diverse fields have in turn supplied Israel with its military leaders. This is certainly no accident. It is safe to affirm that in every full-time Israeli military man there lies a highly qualified and capable civilian. I for one think this accounts for the brilliance of our officers' approach to military affairs.

The permanent Defence Force forms a tiny nucleus of top strategists and technicians, administrative and training personnel. Israel cannot afford a huge military establishment and, anyway, we have found that the reserve system of having on call a highly trained force of most of the able-bodied men and women in the country ultimately works better. Every Israeli in good health, whose religious beliefs do not preclude it, enters adulthood with two or three years of military service. Then he or she goes back to normal life for three-quarters of the time, with the other quarter devoted to reserve training. The result is that at any moment of the day or night the butcher, the baker, the office receptionist or stenographer, the farmer, the university professor, the shopkeeper, the Israeli man and woman in the street can grab a rifle, or hop into the driver's seat of a tank or behind the complex control panel of a sonar listening device and be ready to perform his or her military duties with utmost competence. In that sense, Israel's Defence Force functions as the Swiss military system which also makes soldiers of its citizens; or even more to the point in these difficult times, as the Minute Men of the American Revolution who in seconds could exchange farming implements for rifles in the cause of their country's freedom.

In our preparedness and in our innovations, we go further than other nations. We are obliged to. For one thing, we constantly face the realities of combat. For another, we believe in the equality of men and women and in the fluidity of our officer corps which is based, as I have said, not on class or even education in the ordinary sense but solely on performance.

Here, by way of example, is a typical tank crew as it served in the Sinai during the June 1967 war: a Tel-Aviv lawyer, originally from Germany; a baker from Jerusalem born in Algeria; two Sabras, or home-grown Israelis, one a bank clerk and another a kibbutznik; an electrician recently emigrated from Salonika in Greece. Which one is the officer? In a European Army it would be the lawyer, since he belongs to the traditional class supplying reserve officers. Or perhaps a Sabra boy since they are native Israelis. In the case mentioned, the officer was none of these but the electrician. Why? Because his military performance indicated that he was the member of the group most capable of leading. He might speak with an accent in Hebrew and not have the grasp of Israeli social habits that his native-born companions could display, but the Army is judging him not on these elements or on his civilian status so much as on the talent he has shown in the field.

A commission carries few privileges, heavy responsibilities. During the storming of the Golan Heights in June 1967, the majority of our dead were young officers. That is tragic for all concerned, including the Army and the nation. But in that part of Israel, our farmers no longer plough their fields under the eye of a Syrian fortress with its battery of heavy artillery, but under friendly watch of pioneer kibbutzniks who are building peaceful new communities atop these hills that previously spelt potential death to all who laboured below.

In the Israel Defence Forces, the formal military hierarchy is quite relaxed – shockingly so to European trained militarists. It can afford to be since commanders are hand-picked and outstanding enough to call up willing obedience from their men. Far more important than rank is team spirit. The Hevra, or 'team', with its fierce one-for-all and all-for-one relationship, is a vital element in Israeli military life.

I think the citizen aspect of the IDF makes for both imaginative thinking in military affairs and for exemplary conduct above and beyond the call of duty. I shall give two examples.

During the Sinai campaign of 1956, our Air Force still left much to be desired. We were very short of adequate aircraft. But not of fighting spirit. One tiny Piper Cub plane belonging to Israel held off an Egyptian MIG jet fighter in aerial combat for ten whole minutes before the Israeli went down in flames. The end was inevitable given the disparity of force. That the Egyptian was hounded for so comparatively long a time is a remarkable testimony to our pilot's flying skill. And that he stuck it out in such unequal combat is an example of courage before which one can only bow as a true case of David confronting Goliath. That pilot's conduct is typical.

As for initiative, I recall the brilliant coup pulled off by our Combat Engineers in 1949 when the Egyptians had grabbed our assigned area of the Negev. The Engineers, strong in their knowledge of history, uncovered a forgotten Roman road that enabled us to creep up on the enemy and take him by surprise. We eliminated the Egyptians, lost few lives in doing so and added their armoured equipment to our still meagre stock.

Our staff thinking is 'civilian' in that it refuses to be trammelled by military convention. In most armed services, officers spend much of their time sitting out their contemporaries in an endurance match for promotion. They have no incentive to be original and every cause to avoid sticking their necks out. In Israel time-serving is an irrelevancy. The General Staff prides itself on seeing military problems from fresh angles.

One of the freshest of those angles has turned out to be the most ancient. Our strategists are deeply immersed in the Bible and go to it regularly for information concerning local terrain and also for lessons in tactics.

Because of the strategic problems facing a country that even today is in some places only fifty miles wide, our Forces have had to innovate in all kinds of spheres, from special attention to extreme mobility to the stretching of supply lines through all manner of rough and uninhabited terrain. We have evolved new materials and totally new methods for conducting defence under our special local conditions. And the General Staff has had the elasticity to adapt to these conditions that comes from not taking its military status in too hidebound a fashion.

The IDF has been instrumental in stimulating Israeli industry to respond to our war needs. Of course, it's too bad that we have had to develop local industrial proficiency through the pressures of war. The fact remains that now we are advanced in such highly technical fields as aeronautics and rocketry. Today, we repair our own fighter planes and commercial airliners, manufacturing spare parts in our own machine shops. For our size and newness this makes us uniquely independent of the major industrial powers. We can now also build much of our terrestrial military equipment ourselves. This again is due to the imaginative national effort that the Israeli people as a whole have devoted to defence.

A word about women in our Forces. Israel's womenfolk enjoy and exercise equal status and responsibility with men in every activity of life. Their contribution to the development of this country has always been made on a basis of total equality. During the days of Hashomer and through the War of Independence, girls fought alongside men – just as civilians fought alongside soldiers. In the underground, women undertook many perilous assignments. Many died heroically, in the burning wrecks of Palmach's vehicles along the road to Jerusalem, for instance. However, as soon as it became possible to do so, women were taken out of the front-line units.

They perform several vital functions in military life. Firstly, they replace men in non-combatant roles which helps keep our front-line units up to strength. Then too, their service helps fashion in the Israeli mould great numbers of girl immigrants from the less developed countries who must be taught our attitudes of independence, self-reliance and civic consciousness. At the same time, the presence of women is calculated to remove the misconceptions about the opposite sex that new immigrant male soldiers may bring with them from the societies and cultures of their origin. And psychologically, I am informed, men tend to work harder and are more reluctant to show fatigue in physical tests and manoeuvres where the girls keep going.

A remarkable voluntary force connected to the military is Nahal, which was established during my early years as Prime Minister and Minister of Defence. In a sense, Nahal takes up where Palmach left off. It appeals to the same adventurous and public spirited element in our youth. Nahal was an initiative I favoured greatly because it echoed the pioneer experience of my own generation. I must confess, however, that with all my abiding faith in young people I did not foresee the attraction it would exercise over the years and the dimension of importance it would come to occupy in Israeli life.

Nahal combines military service with the pioneering life that is still so essential to Israel's future if we are to develop the huge proportion of wasteland that constitutes our national territory. Every Nahal member is a volunteer. Most come from Gadna, a paramilitary youth organization, also volunteer, drawing its adherents from the fourteen- to eighteen-year-old age group. Gadna and Nahal youth are from every strata in Israeli society. Many, of course, are kibbutzniks, raised in the pioneering ideal. But others come from our cities, some from well-to-do families and some from immigrant backgrounds with no material assets other than the determination to start a new and fruitful life here. Nahal recruits meet for the first time at the age of seventeen. They spend a year going off on camping expeditions and military type manoeuvres. Then, at the time military service is due to begin, each prospective member decides whether he or she wishes to continue with the organization. By this time, each candidate knows the group he or she will serve with and upon deciding to join Nahal, enters military life with that group as a team. The team itself alternates between military training and kibbutz service. In the military these young people receive advanced and specialized commando training. On the kibbutz, they learn everything from farming to the administrative problems of collective living. Then, once trained, and still under military jurisdiction, the Nahal group either joins a frontier collective or goes off to set one up on its own in an area too exposed, dangerous or difficult for normal civilian habitation.

At the end of three years, the Nahal group becomes civilian and the members are free to leave. However, most choose to stay and a new Israeli settlement begins an autonomous existence. Nahal kibbutzim constitute well integrated, closely knit social groups and, of course, they are equipped and ready to assume the tasks of self-defence. Our experience of Nahal proves that its members make first class farmers and first class fighters. They have a brilliant military record in the Sinai campaign and in the Six Day War. I regard Nahal volunteers as the supreme example of public spirited youth. It is they who can ensure Israel's pioneering future and the flowering of what today is desert land.

When I was Prime Minister and also had the Defence portfolio, I made a point of visiting the troops in the field regularly. Not only did I feel obliged to view the situation with their eyes but also the contact with these wonderful young people gave me insight into the Israel that was coming to pass and that I had worked for all my life. For here was the future. These youngsters, after a year or so of military service, were becoming true Israelis, a new being different from their parents or the pioneers of my own day. With the adaptability of youth, they seemed to spring from this soil even if only recently arrived. They were of the Middle East with a mentality apart from that of Europeans, Americans, South Africans, the ghetto populations of less developed areas or wherever else in the world they had come from. The IDF has succeeded in moulding a new youth in which the best of the old has married a pride in oneself as a person, as an Israeli and a Jew who exhibits far closer links with the Biblical inhabitants of this land than with today's Diaspora mentality.

Because we have had to call on every able-bodied male up to the age of forty-nine and every able-bodied woman up to age thirty-four, many of our field forces have been newly arrived immigrants from every conceivable background. For this reason above all, I rate the armed forces as so great an accomplishment. They have become a training ground for integration into the national community. As a teaching instrument, the military ensures that aside from combat training, every recruit leaves service with a knowledge of Hebrew, the Bible, Israeli and general history, geography, mathematics and civics, bringing him or her up to the minimum standard of education in this country. Further, in the military no distinction is drawn between the ignorant and the more educated, between Sabras and immigrants who in civilian life may have unfortunate but inevitable barriers separating their spheres of activity. Thanks to the military, an illiterate young man with feudal ideas of the social order, who looks upon women as chattels to be sequestered in the home and so forth, can find his place in the twentieth century and in our very up-to-date society. I repeat, therefore, that were eternal peace to come today, and we could all safely throw away our uniforms, scrap our weapons, we would still require an institution devoted to peaceful ends that would take over this melting-pot, educational function of national service so that the younger generation would profit from the unforgettable experience it provides.

Having made this quick survey of the military and its role in Israeli life, it is easy to see why our particular approach to defence is no threat to democracy.

Quite apart from other factors, the IDF depends on common consent of a high order. This can only be given freely in a democratic spirit where authority emanates not from a rule book or a decree but from a desire for proficiency and emulation by example. You cannot have a volunteer outfit like Nahal thrust out on its own, often in the teeth of the enemy, without relying on a spirit of dedication and an equality among men that feeds on democracy and that in turn democracy feeds on. No, ours is a civilian force that in its every manifestation bespeaks of individual consent given for a higher good.

The Israel Defence Forces, then, have a fine fighting record, as all the world appreciates. They have played a formidable part in integrating the different immigrant groups into our community. They have introduced thousands of young women and men to a life of pioneer farm settlement. They have proved themselves a great instrument for education. That they emanate from a democratic spirit is further underlined by the fact that Israel is almost the only country in the Middle East where the military plays no role whatsoever in politics. Here it is conspicuous by its absence. And this is a most important substantiation that the IDF sees itself solely as an instrument of the State, the elected representative of the people. To inhabitants of the old, established democracies this is hardly startling. But, like democracy itself, it is, I believe, quite an achievement for a young State conceived in turmoil and to this day surrounded by enemies.

As Prime Minister, I met representatives of many countries with whom we had dealings, and I know how impressed they were with Israel's achievements in its comparatively short period of nationhood. They were taken, as they said, with Israel's creative drive, its spiritual strength, scientific advances and with such original forms of collective living as the kibbutz and moshav co-operative farm settlements. They would comment favourably on the unique pattern of our labour movement and the functioning of the co-operative idea in so wide a range of activities as building, road construction, housing, health services, even banking, in addition to the more usual consumer and marketing co-operatives. These new and original social forms are attractive to many developing countries in Africa and Asia that have been trying to introduce them at home with our help. But more than anything else, visitors would tell me how especially impressed they were with our military exploits. They would come specifically to see what manner of people could hold out militarily against such heavy odds. They discovered that the co-operative spirit they had observed in other institutions was also very much a part of the Defence Forces. And they would tell me how much of a piece the IDF appeared to them to be with the spirit that had built the State and created our novel human associations.

It is because the military emanates from the State and because it embodies the best in us as an instrument not of aggression but of defence that I say it can be no threat to but only an upholder of democracy.

7 · 'The Bible is our Mandate'

The words are David Ben-Gurion's to the British Royal Commission of 1936. Under Lord Peel, the Commission investigated growing tensions in that barren little territory of rocks, sand dunes, salt flats and waste that the Romans had re-named Palestine, so as to wipe away all memory of a people it had cost them dear and taken them a humiliating time to vanquish.

On the one hand, Lord Peel and his colleagues examined the situation of 800,000 Arabs living in age-long poverty, illiteracy, disease. Recently, their spiritual leader, the Jerusalem Mufti, had roused them to a vision of salvation through violence.

The Commission had also to consider the case of 650,000 people representing the country's oldest surviving inhabitants. A few of these could trace their family genealogy through four thousand years of physical attachment to this soil. Most, however, had returned in recent times on the imperative of an abiding dream. The ways of this people were peaceful and as such bore the contempt of Islam. A Moslem saying, meant to be derisive, had it that the Jews busied themselves with 'bringing trees and birds to the land'.

Ben-Gurion's statement that the Bible constitutes a Mandate bore witness to a concept informing Jewish life throughout the era of dispersion. During nearly nineteen hundred years, the Jews had lived in political impotence unable to challenge the alternate waves of turmoil and stagnation sweeping over this perpetual crossroads of human history. But they had maintained their faith that the promised land was here. So they had prayed and hoped and waited passively for a Messiah to lead them home.

No Messiah but nineteenth-century positivism as coupled to Biblical affirmation of the Jews' historical place in the land of Israel prompted their massive return. Once arrived, they sought redemption from long exile by digging out the rocks from the soil, blasting away the salt, draining the malarial swamps, irrigating the waste and generally obeying the injunction of their prophets to 'make the desert flower as the rose'. Today, the double title of labour and history is taken for granted by the native-born generations. Their affinity is far more with the distant past of sovereignty than with the period of exile. In school, they study the wisdom of Jeremiah in much the near contemporaneous spirit with which Americans consider the utterances of Abraham Lincoln. The theological involutions of Talmud seem more remote.

That the Royal Commission accepted the fact of Jewish settlement is attested by its famous report confirming the Balfour Declaration of 1917 and pressing upon a reluctant British government the necessity and the right of the Jews to an independent national home in their ancient land.

By 1936, the Jewish people had powerful and material justification for claiming their part of Israel. But the historical arguments for their presence were and are today no less significant.

Archaeological evidence uncovered in this century indicates that, with the Chinese, the Jews share the distinction of being the oldest bearers of human civilization surviving to our day with cultural traditions and language intact. Judaism, a foundation stone of Western ethics, consists of three, basic inter-related elements: belief in a single Almighty God, the first such monotheism to be adopted by any people in history; an area of land considered uniquely and especially the heritage of the Jews; a sacred Book recording both the belief and the presence in Israel that affirms the territorial link.

Torah, as again confirmed by modern archaeology, takes up in about 1900 B.C.E. the epic of the people who much later – at the time of the Kingdom of Judah – became known as Jews. Their appearance on the historical scene coincides with that of the first known Chinese dynasty, the Hsiah Kings. The Book tells of the nomad Abram from Haran in Mesopotamia who becomes a 'Hebrew' by crossing to the *less civilized western bank of the river Euphrates. It follows his wanderings southwards through the Zion hills and Negev wilderness in the sparsely populated back country regions of Canaan. Here, as Abraham, 'Elected of God', he preaches his philosophy of the universal Almighty. And here, so Torah records, he declares that Canaan shall be the abode of his descendants, the Hebrew people, who shall consecrate it as the Land of Israel, meaning the 'Land of the Championship of God'. Thus from its origins the Hebrew tradition and Israel are associated in symbiotic relationship that to both brings fruition. From that time on, the bond between the Jews and this area remains unbroken.*

Moreover, the Jews are the only inhabitants of Canaan-Israel since the time of Joshua, in the fourteenth century B.C.E., to prosper in this place and to make the earth prosper.

Here, too, they elaborate their Bible so that, while its ethical message remains universal, it specifically tells the story of a single people whose destiny it associates indissolubly with a mountain top, a desert wilderness, a capital city, a geography. This geographical anchor by its very concreteness gives substance to spiritual ideals and thus helps endow the Jews with the intellectual and emotional force to endure exile as a people. Ultimately, then, one can consider the Bible as responsible for the Jewish presence in modern Israel. In this respect it is a Mandate. Nothing better illustrates the unyielding belief in redemption through physical return to the homeland, as inculcated by the Book, than the traditional saying of the Jewish people through the whole of their wanderings whether as exiles in Babylon, in bondage at Rome, during the Inquisition at Toledo, in Lublin under Cossack persecution, or twenty-five years ago at Sobibor, Belzec, Chelmno, Majdenek, Auschwitz and the rest: 'Next year in Jerusalem!'

FROM when can one date the Jewish return to Israel? Certainly not from 14 May 1948, our formal Day of Independence. Notwithstanding subsequent battles to maintain our State, this event merely recognized an accomplished fact. Perhaps one should consider the Balfour Declaration as the suitable landmark. Hardly, since Lord

Balfour based his words on the visible results of a fifty year
Jewish effort to settle and pioneer what was at that time a desolate territory. In 1917, the Jews were already to be reckoned
with in this country. So we must go back further. Should we
take the establishment in 1870 of the first modern Jewish institution, the agricultural school at Mikweh near Jaffa, as the date
of return? But what provoked the building of that school in
a wasteland? What provoked the first wave of pioneers,
socialists all, to call themselves the Bilu Aliyah with Bilu
standing for the initials of the Hebrew phrase: 'O House of
Jacob, Come let us go up?' It was always the same dream,
always the same yearning for the one place on earth the Jewish
people call home. And the Bilu pioneers, important as they
were in our modern history, weren't the first or only Jews
here. Always some of our people, twelve thousand or so, had
represented us in this area.

The First Aliyah arrived in a country of empty spaces and
slums. Jerusalem was a crumbling village where hovels alter-
nated with monuments gone to seed. The soil of the territory
called Palestine was almost bare, its main inhabitants nomadic
tribes wandering without respect of boundaries across the
more desolate reaches of the Middle East. The American
author Herman Melville, who on a visit to the region
actually saw Bilu settlers coming off a ship at Jaffa, wrote at
the time: 'Here is the implacable nudity of desolation.... No
other land could dissipate so quickly the romantic expectations of the Jews.... In the vacuum of Jerusalem's dead
antiquity, the Jewish immigrants will be like flies who have
elected to live within an empty skull.' How unfortunate
that Mr Melville cannot return to Jerusalem today!

When the settlers of the 1870s and 1880s arrived, they found
as I have said, a nucleus of fellow Jews who had come at various times in history. A few had always been here. Some had
returned with the religious scholars of the sixteenth century,
Joseph Karo and Isaac Luria, who created a city of mystics in
the mountain town of Safed. Others, the Masoretes and

scholars of Tiberias, had migrated back in the ninth and tenth centuries. Earlier than that, the rabbinate of Jabna had kept the Jews oriented towards Israel. In fact, whenever the Jewish people despaired or threatened to collapse as an entity they were rescued by their tie to this physical place and its inter-action with their beliefs as embodied in the Book and the Hebrew language.

One can say, therefore, without being accused of mysticism, that the Jewish return to autonomy in Israel really dates from the fall of Jerusalem and Masada in the eighth decade of the Common Era. In other words, from the moment of conquest, bondage, expulsion, the Jews dedicated themselves as a people to return. All of Jewish culture strained towards that end.

There is a corollary to the above assertion. From the time the Jews ceased to rule here, no other people were able to make anything of Israel. This is not a 'patriotic' or metaphysical statement on my part but cold fact. Only in Jewish hands has this country been a true and viable independent State, a 'going concern', as it were.

Before the Jews, the Canaanite tribes were prosperous along the Mediterranean seaboard and there were a few interior settlements. But the Hebrew arrival brought importance to the Negev and hill area. From Joshua's time on, the history of the Land of Israel was one of steady development. That development always stopped abruptly when conquest put an end to Jewish power. The Persian Emperor Cyrus was well aware of this and in the interest of his own economy he vouch-safed the first return to Zion after the Babylonian occupation: 'Thus saith Cyrus, King of Persia . . . the Lord, God of Heaven . . . hath charged me to build Him a house in Jerusalem, which is in Judah. Whosoever there is among you of all His people – the Lord his God be with him – let him go up.' (II Chronicles XXXVI, 22–23 and Ezra I, 1–3). So the second Temple was built by Ezra and his followers. The Jews flourished once more as did the country at large and the capital of Jerusalem first established under David. By the Roman conquest, this was one of the most important areas of the civilized world.

The Romans laid waste land and city. They spread salt on the earth round Jerusalem as they had done at Carthage. And, as at Carthage, they changed the name of the territory to wipe away all trace of the inhabitants. In a sense, it was a compliment. The Romans only went to such extremes of petulance with foes who thwarted them mightily. That tiny Judah should share the fate of powerful Carthage is a distinction, albeit a dubious one.

In any event, from then on, this part of the Middle East declined steadily. Various invaders' attempts to revitalize it and make Jerusalem into a capital equal to other great cities of Asia Minor - Baghdad, Damascus, Cairo - came to nought. Meanwhile, each successive wave of inhabitants followed the Roman example of destroying Jewish monuments and desecrating our holy places. That is the one thing those who would supplant us have all had in common. Islam in its arrogance built the Mosque of el-Aksar on the site of the razed Second Temple, of which only the Western Wall remains today. Another Mosque at Hebron covers the tombs of Abraham, Isaac and Jacob-called-Israel. During the twenty years following 1948, when Samaria and a part of ancient Judah, including the portion of Jerusalem where all the historical monuments are concentrated, were under Jordanian rule, Jewish edifices were the targets of Arab frustration. As in East Europe under the Communists, synagogues became slum dwellings and storehouses; the tombstones of the cemetery on the Mount of Olives were used in road construction and for latrines.

Yet, I am proud to say, the first thing Israel did upon taking over these same areas in 1967 was to proclaim its intention of safeguarding the shrines of all religions and of according free access to those shrines for all concerned. We do not use Arab Mosques for latrines. Our sufferings and our Biblical heritage impose upon us a code of civilized behaviour which respects the beliefs of all men.

No matter what ignominies the Jews were subjected to, they never forgot their land and they refused to die off. Now our soil blossoms again just as it did in the times of the first and second Temples. Whenever the Jews have been sovereign in Israel, the earth has burst forth with life. And each time they have forsaken it, it has withered and lain barren.

The Jewish relationship to Israel is double, a dialectic. We work the ground and the ground works on us. Here we contributed a universal message to mankind for here the earth gave us sustenance while delivering itself into our care. We have cared for it, continue to do so, as we have for no other anywhere.

There are Jews in America who went there in the earliest days of colonization. Some, especially in the West and in Minnesota, became farmers and even pioneers. Yet the Jews remain an ethnic minority there and those who have a connection with the soil belong to an American ethos, not a Jewish one. In other places, notably in Argentina, the Jews tried cultivating the land. Once they talked of building their national home in Uganda. But these projects and initiatives failed. In the end, outside Israel, we either lost our Jewish identity through assimilation or ended up in the overwhelming majority as essentially a rootless, alien group. We became shopkeepers, middle-men, intellectuals – fine activities in themselves, no doubt, but outside the mainstream of any national existence. The Jews in their practices and beliefs remained foreign to the environments they lived in, objects of curiosity and concern, and only a few years ago of 'special treatment' in the Nazi sense, human aggression towards the stranger being what it is.

Since 73 B.C.E., the Wandering Jew has been a stereotype. But never for those who remained or returned here. In the Land of Israel there is no such thing. This is home. And at home the Jew, like people everywhere, digs his soil, builds his abode, fights to defend every inch of the ground he cherishes so highly. And behold, the city that Herman Melville likened only a hundred years ago to the inside of a skull is once more a busy capital.

In this respect, I think with amusement of a reproach levelled against the Jews in Israel by an Arab nationalist. He complained that we don't take siestas and he used this fact to demonstrate the sinister nature of our presence here. He didn't reflect that after two millennia of ruination the tasks that confront us are too pressing and manifold to allow of such luxuries. May the time come when we can afford siestas!

No consideration of Jewish nationalism in Israel would be complete without examining Palestinian claims to the area, to a country and to a nationalism. What of the Palestinian and Arab outcry that this land belongs not to us but to them?

First, our title is older by a matter of four thousand years. Arab nationalism is a phenomenon of this century and I believe that among nationalistic movements, at least insofar as Palestine is concerned, it stands as a cultured pearl in relation to a real one. In other words, Palestinian nationalism is highly artificial, emanating originally from British inspiration. The latter have always depended on the rule of divide and conquer to ensure the good management of their own interests. When it became apparent that the territory under their Mandate was heading for independence, they encouraged the same frictions here between Arabs and Jews as they did between Moslems and Hindus in India.

Be that as it may, the Palestinian 'cause' was subsequently taken up by Arab leaders as an analgesic, a soothing balm to spread over internal problems of development in the surrounding countries which, in the face of governmental corruption, were fated to remain insoluble. Better to turn the thoughts of the people to Holy War than to have them start worrying over their own chronic poverty.

Honest Palestinians make no bones of the Arab failure to develop this land and their traditional indifference to it as a national entity. I was interested to read the statement of a violently pro-Palestinian native of this area who says quite openly: 'My mother and father were peasants. But peasants such as one rarely finds in today's world. . . . They lived the tenth century in the middle of the twentieth. They and their ancestors had changed neither their dress nor their ways in all that time. . . . They were aware of automobiles, electricity, and even refrigerators. But their souls were asleep and the technical advances that they assimilated through instinct served more to freeze them in the past than to bring them into the present.' The writer continues: 'For the people of the region, used to living for six centuries under someone's dominion, one ruler or another was a matter of indifference. . . . At a few kilometres from Jerusalem we lived an almost animal existence, far from civilization.' *

The author of these words goes on to accuse the Jews of tearing the Arabs from their soil and committing atrocities during the War of Independence. I must answer these charges and will do so later. But here they are irrelevant to the point I want to make of the total neglect and passivity towards Palestine as a country displayed by its Arab population. In all the centuries of their existence on this earth, the Palestinian Arabs remained at the most rudimentary levels of human existence. The above testimony shows how they failed to cultivate the soil according to any general plan or indeed develop any sense of national integrity. That each individual Arab villager, as distinct from the considerable nomadic population, was attached to his own house and plot of ground I readily believe. Those Arabs who refused the enemy their collaboration and who didn't heed the Arab Powers' exhortations to flee in 1948 are today cultivating that same land in security and tranquillity, as citizens of the only democracy to put down roots here since the Twelve Tribes!

I well realize the love every human being may feel for his particular piece of earth. But that the Arab Powers and the so-called Palestinian nationalists of twenty years after should claim in our time that the Arab population here has ever

* Edouard Saab writing in *Les Deux Exodes*, Editions Denoël, Paris.

thought in terms of a country or has laid title to this land as an entity is not to be considered seriously.

If one would need further confirmation of this lack of true nationalist feeling, the military record supplies it. Like the Egyptian Fedayin, the Palestinian Arabs have shown little tenacity in open battle on this soil. The Jews are known to fight with passion, with all the strength they possess. Each Jewish soldier has a deep personal commitment to defending this country which is his home and the only one he knows he will ever have. The Palestinian Arab shows no such emotional involvement. Why should he? He is equally at ease whether in Jordan, Lebanon or a variety of places. They are as much his country as this is. And as little. He doesn't really think in terms of countries! When it comes to the moment of truth in open combat, the Jews display a fortitude born of desperation and defensiveness while the Arabs often enough throw down their weapons and run, or surrender. I could cite case after case where this has occurred, even when the Arab forces have been numerically stronger and better equipped than our own. But why should an Arab fight for this place? Because of specious propaganda attempting to prove his attachment to a mythical Palestinian nation? Propaganda is not worth dying for and deep in himself he knows it. The question is not one of bravery or cowardice but of conviction. The Arabs don't take their nationalist pretensions to Israel seriously enough on an individual basis to stand firm at the front. The Jews on the other hand know that either they defend themselves or the whole meaning of their lives will be destroyed. The conduct of Arab troops in the field since 1948 proves the lack of personal involvement with which the individual fighting man approaches what one can only term the fantasy of a nationalistic claim to this land.

Certainly to compare the 'nationalist' outlook of Palestinian Arabs to the Jewish ideal of Israel doesn't make sense. It's like judging oranges in terms of lemons. The two feelings, concepts, views of this region and its meaning to each inhabitant are not comparable and cannot be meaningfully discussed in the same terminology. One outlook is individualistic and rooted to a piece of small personal property. The other is generalized and attached to the idea of a whole comprising a formal State. The latter I think of as true nationalism, the proof of its validity being that it did in fact produce a State. The former is love of a personal possession. Laudable as that sentiment may be, it didn't and it couldn't build a nation. Nobody, least of all the Jew, wants to steal Arab property. But we do assert the truth that our love for this land in its entirety is the only nationalism that since the time of Canaan all of history, including twentieth-century history, records concerning the region we now know as Israel.

By this I do not wish to deny the recent stirrings of a pan-Arabic movement whereby these peoples have begun to take cognizance of themselves as a totality. I believe in ethnic relationships and in the consciousness of peoples for their affinities. How could I do else as a Jew who has devoted his life to invoking a sense of Jewishness in others of my people? Pan-Arabism could be a great force for good in the world. Unfortunately, the early glimmerings we witness today have been turned to aggressive and destructive ends. Instead of contributing to a general desire for modernization, democratization and for catching up with the rest of the world, for making use of its vast resources to the benefit of the entire population, for the revitalization of its culture and for improving the lot of its overwhelming number of poor, pan-Arabism has been the excuse for internal power politics aimed at the enrichment of a handful of individuals, an alibi for warmongering, for obscuring the burning issues of the day with the temporary unifications of hatred, and for the aggrandizement of one Arab power at the expense of another. The pan-Arabism of such as the Sheik of Qatar who builds palaces with his oil revenues while his people live in tents, of the Iraqi government whose internal politics resemble the saloon brawls of American Wild West films, or of Nasser whose great ambition seems to be to conquer everything in sight regardless of how it is to be administered and despite his manifest inability to run his own country, is not a very inspiring doctrine to the outside observer.

Since the advent of Israel, Palestinian nationalism has become the rallying cry of all the Arabs. It is the only subject on which they appear able to achieve a semblance of unity. That this Palestinian need for a nation failed to express itself in any way between the year 636 C.E., the beginning of the Arab penetration into this area and, say, 1936 when the Jerusalem Mufti spun his Caliphate dream, is ignored by the propagandists. In 636, the Jews were yearning for Israel as they were in 1948. Now they yearn to keep it. One has only to look at the land and think of Melville's description to see what the Jewish presence here has meant. One has only to read the words of the Palestinian nationalist I quoted above to comprehend what so-called Arab nationalism produced here: nothing. And, as Shakespeare puts it, nothing will come of nothing. As to the Jews, I can only point to our Bible and to its sequence in the many Jewish initiatives to regain Israel stretching across the centuries since Masada and say: This is our Mandate. Come see for yourselves.

Since I invoke Torah so often, let me state that I don't personally believe in the God it postulates. I mean that I cannot 'turn to God', or pray to a super-human Almighty Being living up in the sky. Recently, I was asked whether in moments of stress I 'commune' with God and I shocked my interlocutor by asking him back: 'Does God have a telephone?'

Yet, though my philosophy is secular, I believe profoundly in the God of Jeremiah and Elijah. Indeed, I consider it part of the Jewish heritage and the Jewish obligation to hold to this concept of God. Consider Elijah's famous revelation at Horeb:

And Elijah went forty days and forty nights unto Horeb, the Mount of God, where he lived in a cave. And Elijah listened for the voice of the Lord. A great and strong wind rent the mountains and broke in pieces the rock. But the Lord was not in the wind. And after the wind came an earthquake. But the Lord was not in the earthquake. And after the earthquake a fire. But the Lord was not in the fire. But then, Elijah listened very carefully. And deep within himself he heard a still, small voice. And it was so, the voice of the Lord.

Every man has a conscience and the faculty within himself to discern between right and wrong. That is the meaning, at least to me, of Elijah's still, small voice and of Jeremiah's counsel.

I am not religious, nor were the majority of the early builders of modern Israel believers. Yet their passion for this land stemmed from the Book of Books. That is why the socialists of the Bilu movement named themselves with reference to Ezra. And it is why, though I reject theology, the single most important book in my life is the Bible.

Like many Jews, no doubt because of early traditional training, I have a fondness for study. I have read in various cultures, all of which have made me richer as an individual. I learned Greek so that I could enjoy Plato, for whom I have deep respect and who has given me many happy and speculative hours. I have also studied Hindu and Buddhist thought. From Plato, one learns elegance in reasoning; from Hinduism humility; from Buddhism the peace that comes of meditation. But from Torah one principally learns a moral activism that characterizes the Jews and that, I believe, has made them so admired and so detested whenever they have lived among others.

Jewish history in dispersion is a stormy one, ranging to extreme high points and to the lowest depths. In accordance with the dictum that evil outlasts good in human memory, we are particularly sensitive to the continual sufferings inflicted upon us during our two thousand year journey round the civilized world and back to Israel again. But the Jews were also respected of their fellow men. They flourished in Islam for many centuries, helping to guide the destiny of this daughter culture. And they are the architects of Christianity. Who could have been more of a purist in Judaism than Jesus?

Jews are activists, that is they have a Messianic spirit. They are not missionaries since they don't seek to convert others to their ways. But they are merciless with themselves. The Bible has imparted to them that divine discontent leading at its best to initiatives such as the pioneering life, at its worst to persecution by their fellow men. It has never allowed them as a people to enjoy for long comfortable mediocrity.

Certainly in Israel today we are Messianic. The Jews feel themselves to have a mission here; they have a sense of mission. Restoration of sovereignty is tied to a concept of redemption. This had determined Jewish survival and it is the core of Jewish religious, moral and national consciousness. It explains the immigration to Israel of hundreds of thousands of Jews who never heard of Zionist doctrine but who, nevertheless, were moved to leave the lands wherein they dwelt to contribute with their own effort to the revival of the Hebrew nation in its historic home.

A secular vision of the Bible must examine the postulate of the Jews as a Chosen People. I believe firmly that the true situation in history was the reverse of what the phrase implies. I think the Jews chose their God and not, as Torah puts it, that He chose us.

Torah suggests that God consulted the various peoples of Earth and asked, in effect, 'Can you accept my teachings? Can you agree that killing is wrong, that you should not commit adultery?' And so forth through the list of Commandments. The other peoples said no, we said yes and forthwith were adopted by Him.

But that is a mystical conception. The rationalist considers that the Hebrews, as so many other human beings, asked themselves: 'Who are we? Where did we come from? What are we doing here?' Their answer, over the millennia, is embodied in the Bible.

Both Deuteronomy and Joshua make references to the active choosing of God. Joshua assembles the Children of

Israel at Schechem and asks them: 'Who are you going to pick for your God? The God of the peoples among whom you have lived? Or those of your forefathers from across the Euphrates? Or will you give your allegiance to the God I serve?' They answer: 'We will choose your God, the Lord.' But Joshua, not yet satisfied, points out how difficult He is. Nevertheless, say the people, we choose Him. Joshua then calls upon them to state this act of choosing formally and they bear witness to it. So it is clear that the Israelites have chosen God positively.

The uniqueness of the Jews is their adoption in the ancient world of a single invisible and Almighty Being. Such a Being is supreme in a way no surrogate god representing an element in Nature can be. Lesser gods lose their awesomeness by being all too human in their 'private' lives and in their quarrels with each other. In fact, the gods contemporaneous with the first Hebrews are often modest in their conduct. For example, in the Epic of Gilgamesh, discovered at the turn of this century in the excavated library of King Ashurbanipal at Nineveh and dated about 1700 B.C.E., there is a description of the Great Flood and the survival of an Ark very similar in its material details to that in the story of Noah. Archaeologists have, by the way, found actual traces of the Flood but that is another matter. The Gilgamesh tablets describe the gods of Mesopotamia, those Abraham abandoned for the Lord, as terrified by the disaster of the rising waters. They flee to the upper reaches of heaven where they 'crouch and cower like dogs'. One cannot imagine YHWH acting in this way since all Creation stems from Him.

The Greek and Roman gods are famous for either abusing their privileged status to lead the sort of love-life we humans daydream about, or incessantly quarrelling. Usually both things at once. Again, the Jewish God remains above the battle.

Other peoples during the time of Jewish sovereignty in Israel had a hard time grasping the concept of the Lord. The

Greeks considered the Jews godless because, as Alexander noted when he came to Judah, they displayed no idols. The Romans thought us lazy because of the weekly Sabbath when even servants and animals remained idle. They did not understand that the day of rest emanated from God and that the Jews as His tenants on Earth were following His law in seeing to it that all things of Nature within their jurisdiction received due repose.

The Jewish God had fashioned man in His image. This gave the latter, according to the Jews, a special role. God although invisible and endowed with supernatural powers called upon man, His steward, to emulate His example. Thus mankind had something to reach for, an ideal of moral conduct, beyond himself. He also had the freedom to utilize the products of Earth to increase his dominion over Nature and himself.

The Bible is universal in its message of love and of the oneness of man. I have already remarked on its remarkable aspect of starting with the beginning of the universe rather than with the Jews themselves. Torah is not exclusive to a people since it clearly shows how all men spring from the same seed. All women too. This business in Genesis with the rib is, surely, just an afterthought!

Yet Spinoza was expelled from the Jewish congregation of Amsterdam for noting the contradiction: God is said to have picked the Jews to carry His message and to be a special people, a specially good and moral people living in their assigned land. How can the Lord be universal, asked Spinoza, and have a Chosen People? I won't argue the metaphysics of the point. But the message of the Chosen People makes sense in secular, rationalist and historical terms when turned around to describe an act of selection by Abraham and his successor of a God they had formulated. In other words, first came man, then his gods. This does not decrease the power of the Jewish God to work for good nor the validity of the Bible's message of righteousness. The Jews in their Book, according to the secularist idea, set down an accomplished fact by saying: 'It is our duty as a people to be a model to the God we have chosen, to conform to His ways as we have defined them and to devote ourselves to making the land we have settled and attributed to His gift to us a prosperous land run along our moral precepts.' In that sense, the Jews can be considered a self-chosen people.

Unfortunately, no human beings have yet achieved perfection or anything close to it despite good intentions, religious belief and codes of behaviour. The Jews had their ups and downs as a sovereign people. In Isaiah's view, they were the worst people on Earth for a portion of their history. Nevertheless, and this is remarkable, they always produced moralists who laboured mightily to keep them in the paths of righteousness and whose words the Book carefully records. I refer to the Prophets.

A Prophet in the Jewish sense is no oracle. He isn't clairvoyant except through the exercise of his intelligence. He doesn't read ashes or put himself in a trance or predict the future according to magic. No, the Biblical Prophets were men of the world concerned with the daily facts of life in relation to their understanding of God's will. They considered themselves secular critics. Amos, for instance, was furious at being called a Nabi or wandering religious devotee.

The Prophets cleaved to the word of God as handed down in Biblical heritage. They devoted themselves to bringing the peoples' and their rulers' conduct in line with that word.

Amos spread the message of love. He affirmed the equality of man and drew attention to the family tie linking humanity as a whole. Reflecting on current problems in our world, I have often thought that had America heeded the message of Amos it would have refrained from importing black slaves from Africa. Had it not done so, it wouldn't be faced with the terrible problems of ethnic integration that beset it so today. Amos said that none should suffer the sins of the fathers. But Jeremiah pointed out that each man had the ability to distinguish right from wrong and that consequently the act of wrongdoing could call down all manner of long term disasters.

Whether one listens to the one or the other, the fact is the Americans of the present era are reaping a racial whirlwind sown by their ancestors a century and a half ago. Amos's message of brotherhood does have eternal relevance, it would appear. I wish our present neighbours would realize this.

Isaiah developed the message of Amos to thunder against war. He knew that war was self-perpetuating and carried the seeds of destruction for those who waged it. Moreover, he said that if people would stop producing weapons and actively practise peace, they would lose their capacity and taste for bloodshed.

It is a tribute to the ancient Jews, I think, that they carefully recorded the Prophets' outspoken denunciations of their own wickedness. Generally, these critics had a privileged position allowing them to say the sort of home truths to their rulers that normally would put a man in irons or sever his head from his body. And they had their own view of history which without moral conduct meant to them nothing. One of the Jews' most successful monarchs, Jeroboam II, who almost recreated the empire of Solomon, is dismissed by the Prophets with the statement: 'He did what was evil in the sight of the Lord.'

The Bible gives prominence to these thinkers and always discerns the true from the false prophet. There is a dramatic illustration of this in the days of Jehoshaphat I when four hundred false prophets soothed the king by telling him of victory while the one 'true' prophet foretold defeat. In the modern world we know such situations. Too often peoples and governments heed only what they want to hear.

One of the greatest statesmen-prophets was Jeremiah. He lived in an age of decadence and didn't enjoy the immunity of his predecessors. He was a most astute political thinker. Had he been listened to, Judah wouldn't have known defeat by Babylon and the first Jewish reign in this land wouldn't have terminated in war and the destruction of the first Temple.

When the Assyrian Empire came to an end in 609 B.C.E., Babylon and Egypt disputed for supremacy in the Fertile

Crescent, the civilized part of Asia Minor. Jeremiah counselled strict neutrality. His king, Josiah, listened to the blandishments of both empires and over-ruled the prophet. He sided with Babylon and suffered defeat by Egypt. Thenceforth, Judah joined one side or the other as circumstances warranted. But it withstood almost continuous defeat. Jeremiah continued to call for neutrality. He castigated the Israelites for allowing corruption in high places. King Zedekiah tiring of these denunciations threw Jeremiah into prison as a traitor. Zedekiah played politics with Egypt and enraged the Babylonians. The result: Jerusalem was razed to the ground by the vengeful Babylonian ruler Nabuchadrazzar. During the days before disaster Jeremiah, though threatened with torture and death, continued to tell his message of scathing criticism. The people held him in respect for his courage and today he is a symbol of selfless integrity.

The Prophets were perpetually telling the Jews how difficult a people they were in the eyes of God who deplored their deviations from the moral code they had set themselves. These men made many people uncomfortable but always they were respected. And I think they left the Jews with the heritage of striving towards a certain morality, a drive to seek the path of truth wherever it lay, whether attainable or no.

The Jews have always had a conscience. This together with their strict code of life helped keep them true to themselves when they were expelled from their land. It also pushed them to take a prophetic stance, to take readily – sometimes too readily – to the role of critics in the world at large. The Bible endowed the Jews with a self-appointed mission as thinkers, questioners, formulators. Even as they yearned for home in Israel they journeyed across the earth and, in the manner of their Prophets, asked difficult questions. The result was two-ended: exaltation on the one hand, persecution on the other. Their nostalgia turned the majority of Jews in upon their own communities wherever they happened to be. Where they went they tried to re-create the atmosphere of their existence in the ancient nation. But other Jews took their Messianic activism into outside society and either became revered advisers of humanity or society's villains. In our own time, Freud and Marx have been both to a sizeable portion of men.

Without our Book of Books, we might be in Uganda today, or more likely the Jews would be as extinct as the ancient Mesopotamian peoples. In serving as a portable homeland, it has provided a sense of the past. All peoples need their past as a life-giving sustenance and this is the use of history. I notice today that one of the greatest reproaches American black people level at the white man, one of their greatest sources of bitterness, is that for two hundred years they were deliberately cut away from their African past and that they no longer are aware of their own history. This is a cause of rootlessness to the Negro people of the United States and probably a great incentive to the destructive violence they have displayed. If you have no heritage, why respect the heritage of others?

Thanks to our Bible, the Jewish reinsertion into a creative stream of human history, as realized by the return to Israel, has been relatively easy. Our roots stretch deeply into the past. But our lack of sovereignty for so long has made of us a very diverse population with a variety of ties elsewhere and a babel of tongues. Our neighbour, Egypt, on the other hand, can theoretically claim a continuity of six thousand years with a literature going back at least that far. Yet let us look again. The people of Egypt cannot speak the language in which Pharaoh addressed Joseph, and only a handful of scholars can understand the ancient writings of the day. We, however, have kept in touch through Torah with the tongue of our ancestors of 3,500 years ago. Were Abraham himself to return to Israel this day, he might have to spend six months at an Ulpan (Hebrew language school) learning such terms as 'automobile', 'transistor', and 'jet plane'; but the patriarch of patriarchs could ask for his bread and preach the word of his God to his children in this land, and make himself understood!

Our brothers in dispersion often reproach us for reviving

Hebrew as a living language. They cannot understand us, they say. It isn't worth their while to learn a language spoken by so few people, they tell us. Why didn't we make English or German or even Yiddish our official speech, they ask us rather bitterly.

I can only reply that whereas fashions change, history endures. Let me enlarge.

When I came to Israel, language was a big issue. At that time, the overwhelming majority of immigrants were coming from Russia and Eastern Europe. They all spoke Yiddish. So there was a sizeable move to adopt this 'Jewish' language as the official tongue here. Yet, despite the fact that Yiddish really was a *lingua franca* among the Jews of the day, we didn't declare it the speech of Eretz Israel. Why? Because its association was basically one of sadness, of exile, of loss and of persecution.

So others said: 'Let's speak German. It's close to Yiddish and easy, therefore, to learn. And it is universal, one of the great languages of the world.' Had we decided to speak German, we would today be communicating in the tongue of those who destroyed European Jewry. Not only that; while trying to destroy us they successfully destroyed themselves in large measure. Today, German is just one among many European languages and the Germans themselves are all busy learning either English or Russian depending on which side of an artificial boundary they live on. These are the two great tongues of the moment, with English leading the field.

At Independence, it was obvious that English would be the most useful vehicle of world communication. And we were coming to nationhood under British tutelage. We could have decided to make this our national tongue. Of course, by that time the argument was academic since we were all speaking Hebrew and enjoying it.

However, suppose we had become English-speakers. Again, as with German, we should be adopting someone else's culture. We, the oldest civilized people in the West! That would have been ridiculous. And how do we know that in fifty years English won't be a secondary language with Chinese replacing it at the top of the Tower of Babel?

Had we decided to adopt the language of current fashion, we might have found ourselves having to change official tongues every twenty-five years or so. History is a far better guide. So we opted for our natural speech, the language of our inheritance, our sovereignty and our association with this part of the world.

At once, everything became simple. We brought it up to date so that we could discuss problems of microbiology and nuclear physics in Hebrew, and yet at the same time every inhabitant here possessed the tool to unlock the treasure of his culture to its earliest known record. We had in depth what we lacked in breadth.

For this reason I must say to my friends in the Galuth, in dispersion, that it is not we who have lost contact with you by resuscitating our cultural vehicle and making it live again. Rather, it is you who have cut yourselves off from your roots by denying yourselves knowledge of your own language. If there is a communication gap between the Jewish world and Israel, it is up to the former to close it. We are making history, living history. The Jew in Argentina, France, the United States, India, Russia, New Zealand, South Africa and elsewhere is a watcher on the sidelines. Sometimes, as in the Soviet Union or Iraq, he is a prisoner and forced to stay behind as his people advance. That is a personal tragedy, and a tragedy we share since his absence, his inability to contribute to our Jewish life, is a gap that can never be filled – just as the death of six million potential Israelis in Europe is an overwhelming tragedy for us here today.

But life must continue in the face of sorrow and disaster. The Jewish redemption is here and it is now. We are very privileged to live at a time when we are not forced to survive culturally on mysticism and dreams. It is not next year in Jerusalem but today!

The Jews of the world are coming to realize this, and they are making a choice. Many will cease to be Jews, will assimilate into other cultural traditions. We wish them well. But many more will see their link with us and reach over to grasp our hand of friendship. They will learn Hebrew, will come and will cherish their reinsertion into history.

And I am sure that now we are home again, we shall once more be creative as a people. We have already begun to be so. Today, we are in the process of writing a new Torah not only with scribes but with pioneers and farmers, artists and scientists, architects, teachers, engineers, legislators, collectivists, citizens in every walk of life. All speak the language of Moses and even the freethinkers among them study deeply in the Book, the source of inspiration, provider of a past and of a vision for the future. Our new Torah is being written now but its best chapters are still to come. It is my conviction that they will tell the story of our taming of the desert.

8 · To the Negev

*In twenty years of official existence and a century of active develop-
ment, the land of Israel has accomplished a remarkable evolution.
Today, it impresses the world at large in both agricultural and
industrial productivity. Yet over sixty per cent of the country remains
empty desert.*

*This is a fact of Israel's present situation. No one more than Ben-
Gurion realizes how crucially it bears on the future. His abrupt
retirement from politics to a Negev kibbutz has been represented by
some as an act of self-exile, an immurement in the wilderness. That
interpretation is far from the truth. For Ben-Gurion, developing the
Negev is Israel's greatest task and his move there underlines his
determination to participate in this vital undertaking. He has, as
ever in his life, placed himself in the forefront of what he judges the
most significant field of activity. And he has spared himself no effort,
even in his eighth and ninth decades, to set an example for his people,
thereby turning their eyes southward in the great tradition of the
Jewish past, towards a wilderness at once demanding of redemption
and in turn promising the personal redemption of creative effort for
those who take up its challenge.*

*On what is accomplished in the Negev, maintains Ben-Gurion,
Israel will stand or fall.*

I N Hebrew, 'Negev' is the word for south. The Jewish
attraction to the southland wastes, which extend down to
the tip of that Red Sea inlet known in our time as the Gulf
of Eilath, is an old story beginning with the original

Hebrew, Abraham himself. This land of the Negev is the true cradle of Judaism. In its present isolation, it constitutes a national weak point and danger zone. But here also lies Israel's greatest hope for the future.

What we call Negev is an arid waste where high hills coloured dun, red and purple cast their shadows on narrow crater valleys and canyons. This desert stretches northwards to the edge of the fertile coastal plain along the Mediterranean where the Canaanite kings built their major settlements, impenetrable to the Israelites until Joshua's day. Eastwards, the Negev climbs gradually upward towards the cliffs and crags overlooking the Dead Sea. And in the West it merges without change of landscape into the Sinai Peninsula between the Eilath Gulf and that of Suez. The Negev's rainfall is less than an inch a year and the minimum temperature rarely goes below fifty degrees Fahrenheit. Yet today, between Beersheba – the area's largest city located at its northern end – and the seaport of Eilath, southern terminus of an Israeli built road linking Red Sea to Mediterranean, a number of modern communities have implanted themselves and are gradually extending the wasteland's arable portion.

One of these is kibbutz Sde Boker where I came to live in 1953. That I happened to choose this particular kibbutz is an accident. But that I decided to live in the Negev represents a continuation of the ideas I have followed throughout my life and namely the concept that the principal way the Jews can re-claim their ancient land is not by argument or invoking historical precedent but by their labour, that is, by creating an enduring, fruitful home for themselves where previously there was nothing.

I have always realized that if we are to be economically independent and viable under all circumstances, we must develop the Negev. That is why I held out with some tenacity in 1947 for assignment of the area to the Jewish State. Some of my colleagues thought me ill-advised. What did we want with a sand-dune disconnected to the rest of our designated territory and totally lacking in cultivation? The argument that we might eventually need a seaport on the Red Sea which, along with Mediterranean frontage, would make our shores independent of Egypt, or that we could lay pipelines, mine the desert and eventually irrigate it too, seemed very remote at the time. Nevertheless, during the War of Independence, I was particularly concerned with this part of Israel which early in hostilities was invaded by Egyptian heavy armour.

To me, it seemed more important to re-establish our authority over the Negev than even to attempt the rescue of Jerusalem's Old City. As soon as we had the War under control and were in no immediate danger of being overrun in our central plain and main cities, I entrusted the newly organized Army with regaining this occupied territory.

The resolve to take on the cream of Egyptian armour was no light affair. We were still underequipped and, most important of all, we could absolutely not afford defeat since disorganization of our forces would have left us open to conquest by all the Arab armies. I remember telling the Cabinet at the time: 'We have just made the gravest decision since the proclamation of the State.' Yet the Negev was worth it since Israel's capacity to become self-supporting lay in this land.

So, after an Egyptian aggression on one of our supply columns, we opened Operation Ten Sores, a name reflecting our desire to visit a thousand plagues upon those who occupied our territory.

The key to the whole advance, political as well as strategic, was speed. The General Staff must have loathed me as much as they did the enemy during those days as I was always pressuring them to go faster, ever faster. By 21 October 1948, Beersheba of the Seven Wells, where Abraham watered his sheep and Moses in exile had found a bride, became once again part of Israel. And on 24 October, thanks to the brilliant work of our combat engineers who traced out routes across the desert and cleared emergency roads to transport armour through the area, we encircled the Egyptians by a pincer movement and forced their surrender.

Following the 1949 Armistice I immediately sent the military engineers back to the desert where they constructed roads through this difficult terrain to provide vital transport links with the rest of the country. The most famous of these is the Aravah or 'pioneering' highway from Beersheba to Eilath.

In those early days we had much to do just to start functioning as a country and the Negev couldn't come as high on the list of priorities as I would have liked. All the same, it was a constant concern to me. I deplored the fact that for one reason and another – mainly political – the south had known no Jewish pioneers as had the Galilee. Our country's development was such that the main population crowded together in the narrow strip between Tel Aviv and Haifa with only a relatively few settlements straggling north into the Galilee and almost none southward to the wilderness. Obviously, a fertile strip at that time but nine miles wide in some places, would never be able to survive autonomously for very long. We needed a large and firmly based population in our south. The situation today is slowly improving but this is still a basic need for Israel.

In 1949, the first thing to do was to make the Negev into a 'paying proposition' in immediate terms so that it could contribute quickly to the national economy. We began almost at once to prospect for mineral deposits and to mine in the region of King Solomon's famous copper mines. We also began dredging and constructing the port of Eilath, although access to and from the Red Sea was obstructed by Egyptian occupation of the Tiran Straits. Most important of all, we made use of the Negev's proximity to the Middle East's great oil producing regions by laying a pipeline from Eilath up to the Mediterranean. We reasoned that a good highway plus an oil pipeline could in tandem form an 'overland Suez' that the European oil importers might come to appreciate some day given Arab, and especially Egyptian, political instability as contrasted with our own internal dependability.

The 1956 Sinai Campaign achieved one incalculably great advantage for Israel. It cleared the southern gateway to the sea by liberating the Tiran area. Thus it gave our country access to shipping on a worldwide basis and independent of Suez.

Sinai was the strategic work of General Moshe Dayan who is a gifted member of that generation which today is coming into its own politically. Afterwards, he resigned from the General Staff and came to me saying he was anxious to join the political battle. I had discerned in him a very fine analytical mind. But I wasn't convinced then of his political maturity. I told him so quite frankly. 'Dayan, don't be in such a hurry,' I said. 'Wait a while. Bide your time and learn. Then you won't make mistakes.'

He understood and he has held himself back with what I know is an effort of self-discipline. He has served a very fruitful political apprenticeship and today I believe he would make a Prime Minister of stature.

Our Sabras like General Dayan – they are named Sabras after the Negev's desert cactus – are the most precious resource we have. We must call on them to help guide the destiny of this country. They have first-hand understanding of Israel in its contemporary setting and in its juxtaposition to the Arab situation that constitutes a valuable asset for our political future.

I was telling of my association with the desert. Whereas I had always realized its importance to the nation, my personal experience here came quite by chance. I knew the Negev well and had made a point of travelling through it, reading up on its history and geography. Then one day, when I had occasion to drive to Eilath on official business as Prime Minister, I told the driver to cut off the main road onto a track we had come to out in the wasteland. I wanted to get away from my busy schedule and take a few minutes to feel the vastness of the desert, to renew myself by experiencing the awesome effect, which for me never diminishes, of these open spaces with their message of hope and also of the smallness of men in the infinite universe.

We drove along the track for a bit and suddenly we saw a gathering of people up ahead and a few wooden shacks. We stopped and I scrambled down the embankment to ask these young men and women: 'What are you doing out here?' They told me they were fighting the battle for Israel's independence by taming the wilderness. Since this is what I had been exhorting the Jews to do ever since I entered politics, I was certainly delighted to hear it.

These people also told me they had heard of Tibian settlements in this place some two thousand years ago. The Tibians were a Semitic tribe who communicated in a mixture of Hebrew and Arabic. Said these youngsters: 'If the Tibians could be here so long ago, we can be here now.'

I don't know much about the Tibians and I don't think any people in history settled out here for long. But I do know that making the desert flower as the rose was no mere poetic concept in Biblical times. Where exactly Abraham came from is disputed by scholars. Although Torah mentions Ur of the Chaldees, it is more likely he came directly from the more northern area of Haran in Mesopotamia. In any event, the vast delta between the Tigris and Euphrates rivers was in Abraham's day the cradle of civilization and a blooming garden which archaeology has proved was criss-crossed by a network of artificial irrigation ditches feeding farms and plantations of corn, vegetables, orchards as huge as modern American concerns of this type. These plantations existed for two millennia before the origin of the Hebrews! So the concept of fertilizing the Negev is hardly far-fetched, as it might appear at first sight. And certainly irrigation of vast wasteland areas is not only a modern idea. Let me add that today this once abundant area of Mesopotamia is now an enormous stretch of sand, testimony to man's capacity to destroy his own works and render himself miserable!

I had always regretted leaving the pioneer life and indeed had only done so to represent pioneering interests in the Jewish political movement of the day. I always knew that eventually I would try to get back to a way of existence which to me represents the most satisfying activity open to a Jew. These youngsters had understood instinctively what I had been attempting to drive home to our people: that the Negev was our lifeline, that the struggle for true independence had hardly begun and that it would be won in the desert. So I asked them: 'May I join you?' They were startled but made no objection. At the end of 1953 I took a leave of absence from government and came down here.

The first days at Sde Boker were very hard for me. I was out of physical condition. But the one thing I determined to avoid was any special consideration from my fellow kibbutz-niks. So I had to set myself to keeping pace with the best of them. How tired I was during those early weeks and how I had to struggle not to show it!

The Sde Boker kibbutz followed the normal pattern of assigning work in rotation. Lists of duties and those scheduled to do them were chalked on a blackboard every evening. When I first arrived I checked this board and found that while everyone else was listed by his or her first name it was set down that Mr Ben-Gurion would tend the sheep. Well, I told the others that it wasn't Mr Ben-Gurion who had come to the kibbutz but David, just David. So from then on every day I looked to see what David would do.

My attitude prompted the field foreman to test me out. He gave me some back-breaking chores to handle. I didn't let him know that I knew what he was doing. I worked as hard as I could. How hot it was! Like labouring in an oven. And yet, to tell the truth, I felt a deeper satisfaction with myself and my surroundings than I had in many a year. For me, pioneering is happiness. To be at peace with oneself and to struggle to accomplish work that one believes in and that bears on Nature, what else can one ask of life? In a few weeks

I hardened up and felt ready to take on whatever came my way. By this time I was really part of the group and that, too, was very gratifying. Working with young people keeps one young and keeps one's ideas young. I took great pleasure in sounding their opinions and exchanging ideas with them.

One day at Sde Boker I discovered that the fellow working next to me in the field was the grandchild of a pioneer farmer I had laboured with in the Galilee all those years ago in 1908. What a wonderful continuity! It certainly helped renew my faith in this country and its people to realize that the pioneering spirit could be handed down three generations and bring this boy to the desert. And, of course, I took pride in being fit enough myself to match my work with his own.

I have been asked whether I came to the desert to brood in solitude or in bitterness over the scars of political battle. Let me say first that I have no time for bitterness. Such feelings are beside the point of my existence. I have had close friends and associates some of whose paths have diverged from my own. I have criticized them, not for personal reasons, but because everyone here in Israel, and every Jew in the world for that matter, is part of a vast and vital undertaking, the building of this land. Mistakes are costly both of time and of lives. We can afford to lose neither. So I feel very passionately about the various problems confronting us. My colleagues feel that way too. At times, therefore, our divergences tend to be dramatic. But bitterness has nothing to do with it. I came here first to work, later to think and write. One needs solitude for such occupations. On the one hand, the Negev affords me the pleasure of watching a wasteland develop into the most fruitful portion of Israel by a totally Jewish act of creation. On the other, here I have the peace, the space, the awareness of Nature that I need to give my thoughts and my writings the dimension I want to put into them.

There is much to say on man's need for solitude. I think that one of the greatest assets of our kibbutz system is that although it constitutes a collective, it also has an innate sense of individual privacy. We work together but each man has the time and the occasion to face himself alone. That is most important. I personally have been much on my own and I do not regret it. Quite the contrary. Every human being must reach into himself to find his reason for existing. Now that I am older, I must face the prospect of death. A young man asked me not long ago whether I was afraid of dying. I answered by the Talmudic trick of replying to a question with a question: 'Will it help me if I'm afraid?' I asked him. 'I know I have to die some day. So why should I fear it?' Questions on death deserve to be answered with more questions.

However, I still have much to live for and it is what I always have lived for: my work. The Negev has given me time and perspective to look back on Israel's modern redemption. Nobody else has told the whole story. The younger generation needs to know the background to the present. This will enable them to understand the future with greater perspective. The book I am writing, which I foresee will take another seven years to complete – if I survive to do so – will present Israel as a continuum. In truth, the nation as a viable institution is not really established yet. We've made a beginning, a good one. But beginnings are not enough. That is what we need to tell our youth, and just as with the founders of Sde Boker they will learn from our message of the need for them here in the desert.

My solitude today is of course much deeper through the death of Paula, my wife. During the years we spent together we were truly one, a union of the spirit as it says of man and wife in Torah. Now only half of that which formed my life remains. Her death was a blow not only in its suddenness but also because I always expected to die first. Fate decided otherwise and to that all must submit. Paula was a remarkable woman. She started life with little Zionist or even Jewish feeling. Her background was American. When we decided to marry, I told her she would have to live in Israel. 'I want only two things: Eretz Israel and you. And I believe I shall have both,' I wrote to her in those early years. Because she loved me, she came.

When I enlisted in the Jewish Legion we had been married only a few months and she was already pregnant. When she heard that I was leaving for Canada and there was a chance we wouldn't see each other again, she cried bitterly. She thought that what I was doing was madness. Yet she knew I had to follow my path and she made no attempt to hold me back. I left her with exact instructions as to what to name our child and how to dispose of my few effects were I not to survive.

After the war we met again in Israel and through the years she shared my work, my life, my hopes. Then, in 1953, I suddenly told her we were going to the desert. Again, she thought I was crazy to resign from government and to come out here to live. But she followed me all the same and bravely set about making our home here. I admired her deeply for this. Not many women could have taken such an uprooting so much in their stride. Throughout our relationship, Paula's affection moved me and sustained my life. She had the ability to make my goals her own and now that she is gone life is very lonely. But there is work to do. Even in grief one must strive to accomplish the tasks at hand.

Paula, in her way, understood the call the Negev exercised upon me and must exercise on us all. She would have preferred Jerusalem but she knew in her heart that our presence here was necessary and that this was the setting for the next act in Israel's redemption.

Another point about the Negev. Nowhere, not even in Jerusalem, is the continuity with the past so meaningful as it is here. Abraham's understanding of the Negev and its significance in the life of his people as a part of their Promised Land has great affinity with our view of its importance to modern Israel. He crossed the Euphrates, penetrated into Canaan and moved ever southward. After hunger compelled him to go to Egypt, he again returned to this same area. 'And Abraham planted a tamarisk tree in Beersheba, and called there on the name of the Lord, the everlasting God,' says Genesis (XXI, 33). The simple words combine the supreme concept of God underlying Judaism with the very act of cultivating this barren soil. In sum, Abraham accomplished a consecration of this land to his people and our work follows in his footsteps.

Throughout Israel's tenure, the desert has had its spiritual and economic importance. 'And King Solomon built a navy of ships in Ezion-Geber which is beside Eilath on the shore of the Red Sea in the land of Edom' (I Kings 9–26). And so also King Ahab and his successors had political interests here. Not to mention Moses and the forty years' wandering in this area by the Children of Israel.

Today, it has become vital for Israel to think south, as it were. As I have indicated, we must even out the country demographically. We should seek actively to uproot numerous industries that are far too concentrated in the Mediterranean plain and bring them here. Scientifically, of course, the Negev's very barrenness is a blessing in disguise. What treasures do the sands conceal? We must focus attention on the systematic investigation of forces, known or latent, that can make the Negev thrive. For without the settlement of this region, we simply don't have the 'elbow room' – a term used by the American pioneer Daniel Boone to describe his own need to push ever westward into that continent's unexplored wilderness – to make Israel economically independent and militarily secure. We lack defensive depth. But we can attain it, at least to the point that such concepts still have meaning in these days of aeroplanes, nuclear bombs and missiles, by moving a good segment of the population here and cultivating the land.

Such a move won't be easy. But it will bring the satisfaction of creation. An example from my own experience. When I first came here, we had to pay five dollars for less than a hundred gallons of water because we had to truck it in from Beersheba which is thirty miles away. Now we have a water pipeline coming not from Beersheba but straight from Yarkon which is near Tel Aviv. Today, we have enough water to cover the plateau upon which Sde Boker is located with grass and trees, to sustain livestock and all their produce. In a sense we have created this green spot in accordance with the Biblical injunction that man must comport himself in the spirit of his maker who created the earth.

The desert is a reproach to mankind. It is criminal waste in a world that cannot feed its population. Even for Israel, this barrenness is a reproach. The majority of Jews who come to this country go to Tel Aviv or Jerusalem. I am against big cities. They bring out the worst in men.

It is my belief that every human being is a compendium of good and bad qualities. I think man's capacity to wreak evil, to harm himself, is far greater than his ability to do good. Cities by their anonymity and their impersonality are a nefarious influence on the individual. They remove him from a sense of direct responsibility towards his fellow man. How can you remember to be your 'brother's keeper' in the Biblical sense if you live in an apartment house where nobody knows anyone else? I remember going to New York once with the intention, among other things, of looking up a fellow Israeli who was there at the time. I asked everyone I met about this man but couldn't trace his whereabouts. Then one day in the skyscraper I was living in I bumped right into him. 'I've been searching everywhere for you,' I told him. And he said 'I've been looking for you too.' It turned out we were living in the same building and had been doing so for weeks without either of us knowing it! That is city life for you.

Conglomerations like Tel Aviv are unnatural. They are destructive of the spirit Israel requires to remain true to itself. This country isn't just a Jewish hotel. It's a very special place with special demands on everyone who dwells on its soil. And what Israel has to teach us is far more graspable out on the land and in small communities where each knows his neighbour, where there is community solidarity born of long association and common experience, than it is in a huge beehive of a building jammed up against a hundred other beehives on a long, impersonal boulevard.

Again, the Negev can come into its own as a veritable laboratory for urbanists. We can easily accommodate five million people here. Yes, five million! And in spaciousness, comfort, calm, beauty. We can house them in small enough settlements to allow for survival of the neighbourly spirit. We don't need living areas for more than ten or fifteen thousand in a given spot. And even so, as I say, there's room for no less than five million more. When they have come, when all the people have escaped from Tel Aviv and made their place here, then we won't have to worry about the Egyptians or anyone else shooting missiles at a single location and killing off half our populace.

We need Jews from America, Rhodesia, Iraq, Russia, anywhere they are. We want them to come here and live as free men in a plenitude they cannot enjoy anywhere else both as Jews and as human beings. But here they must work hard to create a new civilization. Not what we have today but something entirely new. We want them to come to the desert and make it different from anything known on earth to this date, fitted to the environment and an inspiration to men everywhere. The more who come, the more will be attracted. In the beginning will arrive the best, the true pioneers, those with the requisite moral character to suffer the hardships out here. This, of course, is already happening.

Israel, I know, will survive on the basis of quality. It is a small state and already it exists because of the quality and fortitude its inhabitants have shown under hardship. Now we require quality in every sphere of activity to carry out the mission of enlightenment worthy of our ancient people. But to get quality, we must have quantity. The more Jews who come, the more scope we shall have to improve our aptitudes and proficiency in diverse domains.

In relation to the desert, I want to see Israel lead the world in taking up such problems as the purification of sea water into sweet water usable for irrigation. The processes must supply the land in large amounts yet be cheap and practical to run. Sounds like a dream. Should Israel be afraid of dreams that can transform the natural order by science, imagination and pioneering? Of course not, for that is our vocation. And the purification of sea water here is not only vital for ourselves but for hundreds of millions in the world who suffer from starvation diets while only a small portion of their available land surface is tilled.

Science depends on the imagination of the human mind and the needs of society. Jewish society needs the Negev and it must bring its people here. This is where a specifically Jewish effort to open the frontiers of the mind and develop the natural capacities of the Promised Land can make its contribution. The supreme test of Israel at this time in its history lies not in the struggle with hostile forces outside its frontiers but in its success in wresting fertility from the wasteland that constitutes sixty per cent of its territory.

Since its expanses were redeemed by the Defence Forces in 1948, the desert has been explored and investigated. Research, however, hasn't gone far enough and latent resources still far outbalance those that have been revealed. Nevertheless, we have already discovered numerous phosphate deposits as well as uranium, gypsum, granite, marble, first quality sand for glass (Israel, by the way, was a glass-making centre of the ancient world), bituminous stone, kaolin and natural gas. Detailed investigation is still required of the flora and fauna, the climate and the dew deposits, the quality of the desert soil and its geological structure.

Then, too, I consider the Negev's great inland lake, the Dead Sea, of tremendous importance though it has been given scant consideration by land developers up to now. It is a unique body of water and lies in the earth's deepest cleft, 1,400 feet below sea level. It is richer in salts and minerals than any other area in the world. It contains about two thousand million tons of potash, over twenty thousand million tons of magnesium chloride, about ten thousand million of calcium chloride, almost a thousand million of magnesium bromide and other minerals. There are probably other resources in the Dead Sea we haven't even thought about. I hear, too, that it is rich in medicinal springs of benefit to health.

To further knowledge of the entire area I have been active in promoting an institution that we have now established at Sde Boker, the College of the Negev. For the moment, it is mainly a teacher's college to train primary and secondary school personnel for the ever growing number of desert settlements. But it is also developing as a research centre where people of every discipline come to investigate this very special region. In time, we hope the College of the Negev will be a prestigious international centre of learning and study on topics connected with the development of desert-like land in general and of the Negev in particular. I hope personally that this College will continue its present policy of being extremely eclectic in its disciplines, where everything from architecture to ecology, from social research to agronomy can be taken up with reference to the surroundings.

The Negev offers the Jews their greatest opportunity to accomplish everything for themselves from the very beginning. This is a vital part of our redemption in Israel. For in the end, as man gains mastery over Nature he gains it also over himself. That is the sense, and not a mystical but a practical one, in which I define our redemption here.

Israel must continue to earn its nationhood and to represent the Jewish people with their awesome past. It must be worthy of itself, which is no small achievement. It is one to be attained in the desert.

When I look out of my window today and see a tree standing there, that tree gives me a greater sense of beauty and personal delight than all the vast forests I have seen in Switzerland or Scandinavia. Because every tree here was planted by us. It was nursed to life by the water we brought to it at such cost and effort. Why does a mother love her children? Because they are of her creation. Why does the Jew have affinity for Israel? Because here again everything remains to be accomplished. It is his privilege and his place to share in this creative act. The trees at Sde Boker speak to me in a special way, in another language than any other trees anywhere. Not only because I helped to grow them but because they constitute a gift of man to Nature, and a gift of the Jews to the cradle of their culture.

9·Peace

Continuing hostility with the Arab world is an overriding concern to every Israeli. And the difficult terms on which the country presently exists are far too evocative for comfort of that equivocal state suffered by the Jews throughout dispersion.

Too often to be a Jew has meant separation from the rest of mankind, existence as a quarry upon whose alien head every aggression and every blame for human misfortune could be heaped with impunity. Israel's rebirth provided an abode the Jews could call their own, wherein they would be strangers no more and from which they could treat with the world in equality. Yet, paradoxically, Israel as a country finds itself quarantined from much of humanity. It is today a 'Jew' among lands, alone and often a scapegoat in the family of nations as its people were alone in their wanderings and often a scapegoat in the family of man.

Persecution is only half the story. Israel is admired as well as hated, respected for its achievements – especially in its social institutions – as well as calumnied for reasons of political expediency or religious prejudice. In this way again, it resembles the latter day history of the Jewish people who in the course of their homeless perambulations often found richly satisfying temporary havens wherein to stop awhile, if rarely permanently. And of the Jews it must be said that harried though they were, their beliefs were adopted wholesale by the western world. In the beginning, as the Bible puts it, came the Word – and the word came from the Jews in their Hebrew tongue. The message was retained as a basic heritage even by those who plagued the authors.

So, too, with Israel whose kibbutzim and moshavim serve, for instance, as the model for a Tunisian effort to develop that country's insufficient agriculture on a collective basis. Tunisia hasn't hesitated to emulate Israeli institutions while deploring the very fact of the State's existence. It must be added that Tunisian initiatives have not met with the success they might have enjoyed had this country's government dared consult Israeli experts in a domain where the latter's direct experience now stretches back more than half a century. But no Arab land can yet envisage the opprobrium of maintaining relations with the Jewish State that the others would heap upon it no matter how profitable for itself such relations might be. So Tunisia's brave attempt to adapt Israeli farming concepts to its own terrain are failing through ignorance and refusal to go to the source of information, Israel itself.

Whether despised or praised, castigated or emulated, the Jews as a people and Israel as a nation suffer from isolation. That is the problem. Yet for Israel, there is no immediate issue. It can only follow its present course which is to survive and develop. Beyond this, Israel must, while yielding nothing to those who would destroy it, grope towards a modus vivendi *with its neighbours. Only in peace can the Jewish homeland come into its own and realize its true potential.*

In considering this goal for his country, Ben-Gurion offers no facile promises and sees no solutions to present problems for some time to come. Yet he is tranquil in the certainty that Israel will outlast and out-build the capacity of its enemies to destroy it and that the day will come when they will arrive at its gates not in hostility but ready to co-operate in a common effort to develop the Middle East's great resources for the benefit of all its peoples.

OFTEN enough, I am asked to predict when and how peace will come to Israel. I am always obliged to give a disappointing answer by confessing that I have no predictions to make. That the situation is highly complex is self-evident, with everything that happens in the Middle East bearing upon the international political scene and, obviously, vice versa.

There was a time when each part of the world functioned more or less autonomously. For thousands of years the great Chinese civilization was unheard of elsewhere and China hardly realized there was anything beyond its Wall. No one in Europe knew of the American Continent or of Australia. On a lesser scale, within the Roman Empire, what happened on far frontiers took weeks to be reported in the capital and rarely was of immediate concern to daily life there.

Today, whatever occurs anywhere is known in hours to a large segment of humanity. The biggest states depend on other states. American problems in Vietnam have repercussions not only on the soil of the nations directly involved but also on Europe, South America and so forth. Events in Czechoslovakia are of vital importance to the Soviet Union as the latter's daily affairs deeply influence its satellites. China still appears to stand alone, unaccepted even in the United Nations. But it well knows its dependence on happenings in Asia, as Asia is aware of the Chinese dragon's innate capacity to swallow up the entire continent.

We are not, unfortunately, living yet in a world united. But we are all subject to the results of what transpires everywhere on the globe. Let us hope our era is intermediary to the achievement of terrestrial unity in peace and not to the destruction of the species. Both courses are easily foreseeable as things stand. An important phrase in the Bible sums up the present situation when it says that all is foreseen by God but man has free choice, the ability to order his life one way or another. Today, the choice is dramatic, perhaps more so than ever before. One needs faith in humanity and optimism to hope that mankind's aggressor instincts will be overcome before they annihilate him.

The Jews have always been optimists. They have had little to make them so during a long and careworn history. Yet they have managed to continue believing in themselves and to emerge from whatever ordeals confronted them with firm hopes for the future. That the victims of Auschwitz could say: 'Next year in Jerusalem,' seems at first grasp almost outrageous in its brightness when the individual must despair. But then one sees the nobility of a statement that denies the enemy his victory while affirming unshakeable faith in one's own. Let us reflect that those who pronounced these words and held to this vision were indeed right, literally so, though they themselves would not live to participate in the home-coming.

Despair leads nowhere. Throughout the millennia of per-secution, the Jews have realized this and never lost conviction in ultimate justice, peace, human equality. I am sure that the Jewish people have hard days ahead of them in Israel. They have overwhelmingly difficult tasks to accomplish and un-doubted black moments to face. But having had the privilege of seeing what they can do when confronting the apparently impossible, I have total confidence in their ability to pass through the shadows and emerge unshaken, present in the land they have struggled so hard and suffered so greatly to regain.

Nevertheless, on a more practical plane, it is my belief that the hostility we face today will continue for some time to come and that we had better reconcile ourselves to riding out the *status quo* as best we can. Our plans for the future are very simple and very pragmatic. We must live on and build the country, receive immigrants and put them to work, extend our education to ever higher levels for an increasing mass of citizens, settle the desert so as to make Israel economically self-sufficient, and utilize every effort, short of undermining our national integrity, to bring about peace.

Eventually, I have no doubt our problems with our neigh-bours will be resolved. New generations are growing up both in Israel and in the Arab lands. These youngsters will under-stand each other better than their parents or grandparents did because they will have so much in common, including roots in the same part of the globe. Will a new crop of Arab young people tolerate the current never-ending conflict in the name of a dubious Holy War whose aims are murky and whose existence compromises the internal development of their own countries? I have too much faith in the healthy iconoclasm of youth to believe it.

There is, of course, the possibility of what one might call 'historical accident', beneficial to the cause of peace. Given the ramifications of Middle East politics the 'accident' of an accord between the Great Powers agreeable to all parties is, I suppose, within the realm of the conceivable, although I for one am extremely sceptical of such an event at this time. I think it pretty obvious that a slackening of Middle Eastern tension would work against Russian ambitions in this part of the world, and against those of other powers as well. Recent efforts to produce a settlement of this nature have been notable only for their total lack of accomplishment.

Yet I see an issue to our troubles in the achievement of world peace rather than by any partial settlement in this area. When will world peace occur? Who can say, except that it had better happen before the alternative event of world nuclear war. It is my guess that in the next twenty or thirty years, if Europe succeeds in being united, peace will have a chance of 'breaking out'. A united Europe could bring it to pass by being a third fully-fledged force in global politics. This would have the effect of drawing the United States and Russia closer together to protect vested interests. Moreover, a Europe united would be a more independent Europe, a third force to balance the other two. It would have every interest in promoting good relations with the whole of the Middle East and contributing to the maintenance of peace in the area.

We are unhappy that the prospects for peace by direct confrontation and negotiation with the enemy seem so remote. But the Arabs are caught in an ideological trap of their own devising. They don't seem able to extricate themselves from the consequences of a disastrous hostility that feeds on itself and assumes quasi-religious significance in its frustration.

If the Arabs were to conquer Israel, one wonders what they could find to do with it. Probably they would turn the clock back a thousand years and let the country rot. There is nothing constructive for them to do here, nothing they truly want or need. The war against Israel has never been an end in itself for the Arabs but merely a Machiavellian tool to obtain some kind of internal and pan-Islamic unity while failing to deal with pressing interior problems. As such, the hostility is in essence mystical, irrational and, therefore, impossible to grapple with on the basis of good will or logic. Every day we Israelis come up with fine rational solutions to the conflict. We'll give a little here in return for a little there and so on. But every day we are hit in the face with raving unreason. Under the circumstances, no direct negotiations are possible.

One of the Arab world's tragedies is that, with the possible and occasional exception of Lebanon, there is no free speech or free press. We cannot really know the nuances of feeling that must exist among the educated classes. We can only know what the rulers think, but they do so in formulae hoping that the populace at large will find comfort in hating us and thus forget the hunger in their stomachs. It's the old Roman idea of circuses instead of bread. For the heads of state, fighting holy wars is so much simpler and more exciting than carrying out the day-to-day drudgery of agrarian and industrial reform, the bootstrap operation of pulling oneself from feudalism into the modern world. Then, too, the paths of peace are fraught with political danger. Developing a country leaves one wide open to constant criticism from one faction and another whose vested interest must be affronted. Far better to dazzle everyone with a cause offering action, uniforms and a way of killing off the unemployed rather than making real jobs for them.

Egypt is the worst offender in promoting this fundamentally self-destructive state of affairs. I blame Nasser more severely than I do any other Arab ruler as I believe he at one time had the capacity, the vision and the means to improve his people's condition and to stop this futile merry-go-round of war. Nasser, I think, had everything but that one essential quality known colloquially as intestinal fortitude, or guts. He can, alas, be compared to Italy's Mussolini who also came to power with excellent potential and intentions but who soon forgot his country's real problems. The Egyptian Mussolini, allowing himself to be seduced by the glitter of Russian armaments – in the manner of a country girl falling prey to a sophisticated city tout – set out to conquer the Middle East. Like the Duce, he didn't get far. Now it's late in the day to scrap the aggressive policies and start over again. Nasser is caught in his own infernal machine whose parts include a commitment to the Soviet Union and its dictates as well as to a population roused to passion against the neighbour whose friendship could be most beneficial to that population's own interests.

One of the most silly and sad things that Nasser has, in my opinion, done to his country is the changing of its name. Egypt, with a history of six thousand years, suddenly doesn't exist any longer. Now it is the United Arab Republic, a land not United, not Arab, nor, for that matter, a Republic. The name change is symbolic. Nasser had it within his power to do so much good. And he used his personal gifts to turn his country from a British colony into a Russian one, to dissipate national energy in wars of conquest that have ended perpetually in defeat. He had the opportunity to go down in history as a great figure of the twentieth century; he has chosen to be a second-rate tyrant whose touch far from turning stones to gold has transformed Egypt's natural capacities to dust. Yet he is the man with whom peace could once have been constructed. That time is long past now and it is useless to regret dictators. One wonders what might have been, as one wonders what can now be Nasser's and his United Arab Republic's fate. This sort of speculation goes nowhere. I can only grieve for missed opportunities. Like past mistakes, they are irrecuperable.

Lebanon is perhaps the only neighbouring country where the situation with Israel is viewed somewhat rationally and consequently with dismay. We always say here that Lebanon will be the second country to make peace. Not the first because this mercantile nation is not known for political daring and it is too dependent on Arab oil money to take a free line. But every Lebanese banker and trader realizes the boost to his own pocket that, under different circumstances, recognition of Israel could entail.

If you look from Israel across the Lebanese frontier you see the same underdevelopment and poverty on the land and in the small settlements as you see in every other Arab country. Beirut is glittering and modern. But Lebanon, too, needs large-scale development. It knows that here Israel could be its greatest helper and that we could also reinforce its independence *vis-à-vis* the oil sheiks.

An incident underlines this affirmation. One of our kibbutzim just a mile or so from the Lebanese border has developed a factory that turns out specialized farm machinery of excellent quality. One day, the head of the kibbutz factory was approached by a man from Cyprus who said he had a Lebanese client wishing to place a massive order for farming equipment. He implied, so I gather, that the client was actually the Lebanese government itself! But, said the intermediary, the machines will have to be shipped from Israel to Cyprus where he, as middle-man, would then expedite them in unmarked crates to Lebanon.

The Israeli factory manager was very amused by the situation. He said: 'I have a much more practical idea. Have your Lebanese client meet me right up here at the frontier which is only a mile from the factory gate. That's much more convenient for all concerned. I'll negotiate any sale he wishes and I'll even pay you, as middle-man, your commission on the deal.' Nothing was ever heard again from either the Lebanese or the fellow from Cyprus. I think the story is, however, illustrative of Lebanon's desire to take up normal relations with Israel and of its awareness of the material advantages such relations imply.

At this point let us change the optic. I want to examine certain criticisms and charges concerning Israel's attitudes towards the Arab situation.

Israel has been accused of profiting from Arab hostility in a variety of ways. The truth is subtler than such a blanket statement indicates.

I think that in some ways Arab aggression has benefited this country. And why not? One has to utilize what is at hand even though the elements themselves might not be favourable or desirable. We didn't create the hostility. We have had to learn to live with it.

One can impute the growth of Tel Aviv, now our largest city, directly to troubles with the Arabs in neighbouring Jaffa. Much more important in my view, the Arab boycott on our goods and the refusal of our neighbours to supply us with agricultural produce forced the Jews to leave the cities on a large scale for the farms. Without that boycott there was danger that we might have built a Jewish Carthage, an urban society ingrown upon itself and dependent on food from other countries. This would certainly have dimmed our hopes for a healthy national revival. Conversely, the boycott of Jewish goods had the boomerang effect on the Arabs of weakening their economies by closing off both a source of supply and a market to them.

Nevertheless, Israel cannot develop under conditions of war to the extent that it could in peace. I think we are the only state in history to have been attacked on the very day of our establishment. Ever since, we have been compelled to give our best youth and brains to war rather than to the workings of peace. This tragedy far outweighs any benefits the condition of permanent hostility may have brought us as a nation.

I have heard it said that were it not for the present tension, Israel would be in danger of disappearing slowly in a 'sea of orientalism' (whatever that means!). I object very strongly to this silly notion and consider it the outcome of slipshod thinking about Israel and its place in the scheme of things.

The Jewish people are not easily overwhelmed. They have their Messianic tradition which binds them together and gives their existence purpose. More than one sea of eastern or western culture has attempted to swallow them up but never has succeeded. They have influenced the world far more than the world has influenced them.

Israel is far better equipped to resist cultural extinction than were the Jewish exiles during two thousand years. Our evident role here is to give new life to all that is meant by the 'Covenant' of the Jewish people whereby they remain one. That is hardly a role leading to 'drowning' in alien cultures. On the contrary, it represents a revival of our own cultural activity.

Most important, Israel is not just an eastern nation or just a western one. It is both! In itself, it unites the two great streams of the Jewish people: the Ashkenazim whose traditions are western and the Sephardim whose cultural links are with the East. Here is another task for Israel: to marry the East with the West and thus again to serve as an example of unity and brotherhood to all mankind. Isaiah knew this when he said:

> I will bring thy seed from the East,
> And gather thee from the West . . .
> Bring my sons from afar
> And my daughters from the ends of the Earth.
> (Isaiah 43–5, 6)

This unification of East and West is of immediate concern to Israel and to Jews everywhere. Our population today comes from India and Finland, Morocco and California, Argentina and Yemen and so forth across the world. There are dark-skinned Jews and fair-haired Jews, Jews who resemble Slavs and Jews who look like Hindus, Jews who come from lands where washing machines, television, telephones, skyscrapers are commonplace, and Jews who have never before lived in houses with flooring. These are the people we are gathering up here in this tiny land. The one thing they all have in common is their Jewish tradition. Far from allowing that tradition to be diluted we must emphasize it strongly as we integrate these disparate groups into our Israeli society.

That integration is going ahead faster than one could have hoped. In part, admittedly, the Arabs are responsible as they have precipitated the creation of our Defence Forces and their unique characteristics. But peace would allow the same dynamic to work for our development and the end result would be even better since we could devote all our energies to labour of lasting significance.

I have called the Arab attitude towards Israel irrational. Nevertheless, the Arab world has levelled several concrete accusations against us and it might be well to answer these here.

They have said, for instance, that the Moslem portion of the globe is paying for Nazism in Europe, that without the holocaust we would never have come here as a mass and never have founded a State. And, complain the Arab propagandists, it isn't fair that this part of the world should pay for the persecutions carried out in Europe.

I have already gone exhaustively into the reasons for our being here, reasons that I as a pioneer of 1906 can affirm have nothing to do with the Nazis! I think that Hitler did much to retard, not advance, our nationhood. In the middle thirties, it looked as though we were soon to achieve a Jewish State. But with war in Europe looming ever closer, thanks to the Nazis, Britain cracked down on Jewish nationalist aspirations with the famous White Paper of 1939. Ripe as we were for nationhood at that time, we had the greatest difficulty in helping even a fraction of European Jewry escape the gas chambers. Certainly Israel's population contains no massive element of direct victims of Nazism or their descendants. We just were unable to save the majority of these people. And those who did escape from Germany and the other countries didn't always come here as we weren't equipped to get them in their hundreds of thousands past the British embargo on immigration or offer them a true nation once they got here.

I would agree, however, that the advent of Nazism and its consequences in Europe did have one direct effect on Israel. It indicated to us all, to every Jew, the potential danger of being without a homeland. Nazism proved that Jews could live for five hundred years in peace with their neighbours, that they could all but assimilate in national society save for a few traditions and separate religious practices. They could believe themselves integral citizens of states professing freedom of belief and granting full rights to all inhabitants. Such was the situation prevailing in Germany, France, Italy, Holland, Denmark, Norway. Yet one raving maniac could blame the world's troubles on a group constituting less than six per cent of Europe's population and the holocaust was at hand!

So, many a Jew realized that to be fully Jewish and fully a human being, and fully safe as both, one had to have a country of one's own where it was possible to live and work for something belonging to a personal cultural heritage. In this sense, Nazism did bring many Jews to Israel, from everywhere on earth. Not as victims of persecution but as believers in the positive good of a Jewish national home.

I have said that personally I was never a victim of anti-Jewish persecution. I have, however, seen and marked the 'outsider' status of the Jews in even the most enlightened countries, as opposed to their full participation in our society here.

I recall a humorous but revealing incident in London during the First World War when I was with the Jewish Legion. I had just arrived and was on a four day leave. They had fed us very badly on the ship coming over and I was looking forward ravenously to a solid meal.

Well, in London there was rationing and I hadn't yet received a registration card. I didn't even know about this formality. As soon as I arrived I went to the first restaurant I saw and ordered a huge lunch from the menu. But the waiter said: 'Show me your ration card.' When I told him I hadn't

one he said that all he could give me was two eggs. I quickly
ate these and asked for something more. All he had to offer was
two more eggs. I ordered these but still felt hungry. By this
time, however, I was getting tired of just eggs. So I left the
restaurant and, wandering around, came across some soldiers.
I asked them where one could get a meal without a ration card.
They said: 'Go to Whitechapel.' 'What is Whitechapel?' I
inquired not ever having been in London before. 'Oh,' said
one of the soldiers, 'that's the Jewish Quarter and you'll find
anything you want there.' I hailed a taxi, had the chauffeur
drop me in Whitechapel and walked along the street until I
found a restaurant. Sure enough, I ate a sumptuous meal with
no questions asked. I left with a full stomach. But I was
ashamed.

Somehow the people of Whitechapel, though calling themselves British, didn't really see the war as concerning them.
They were Jews and no amount of pretence could change the
fact. The problems of Britain, including rationing, were not
their problems. Had there been an Israel and had they lived in
it, these people could not have taken such an attitude. Indeed,
it probably wouldn't have occurred to them to contravene
rationing laws established for their interest and for the good of
their own country.

The British are the most tolerant people I know. I have
come to appreciate them as a people more and more now that
the frictions inevitably opposing Jewish and British interests
under the Mandate are a thing of the past. There is much anti-
Semitism in Britain, but the people are polite enough not to
show it. I remember as Defence Minister interviewing one of
our able young officers who had been attending a course at the
British Military Academy of Sandhurst. When he returned I
asked him: 'How did you get along with the British officers?'
He said: 'They're extremely nice and were very pleasant to me.
Of course, they're all anti-Semites. But they would never
show this to an English Jew.' He said that to him they had been
quite open about this prejudice which didn't extend to Israelis

– precisely because an Israeli was an equal, an opposite number, as it were, from a *bona-fide* country. The British officers explained to him, in effect, that Jews constituted a foreign element in their country's national life and that, therefore, they disliked them, even if they were careful not to show this to their fellow citizens of Jewish origin.

One can only remark that polite or no, the seeds of anti-Semitism remain even in so civilized a place as England. And many a Jew in that country finds it difficult to conform to social norms which are not his own and which he cannot truly feel concern him directly. That is the lesson I learned from these two incidents. From the more violent approach of Hitler and Stalin I was taught that without a place of their own on this earth the Jews are always available as potential scapegoats, a prey for those who would martyr them for political gain.

None of this, however, amounts to the Arab contention that we are here because of Nazism or any persecution elsewhere. We are here in this place because of Abraham and Moses, Joshua and David, the Macchabees, the Prophets and our history. We are here because this land is ours. And we are here because we have again made it ours in this time with the work we have put into it. Nazism and our history of martyrdom abroad do not concern our presence in Israel directly.

Again, the Arabs reproach us with 'genocide', a word much in fashion these days and used loosely by those who hardly know what it means. The Jews have a good grasp of the meaning of genocide from their experience of twenty-five years ago. They also know all about it from Arab propaganda which is disgusting in its hysterical violence and talks incessantly about pushing us into the sea. That we should be accused of having practised the extermination of a people is laughable, especially in the light of all the efforts we have made on behalf of our Arab population.

Israeli policy towards the Arabs has been the diametric opposite of genocide or persecution. We have always played the card of education, enlightenment, democratization. We have gambled that, by showing these benefits to the Arabs who heeded us, they would realize how vitally their interests lay not in fighting us but in allying their ways with ours.

Before taking up the question of Israel's day-to-day relations with the Arabs in its orbit, I should answer the charges made by the Palestinian refugee whom I quoted earlier in another context. He claims that Israel perpetrated atrocities on the Arab civilian population during the War of Independence and pursued a policy of forcing them to depart.

As the Prime Minister of the period, I can state absolutely that this country never by any official act expelled an Arab innocent of plotting against its security. In fact, we took back forty thousand refugees after the Armistice. And we used public funds to help re-unite Arab families within Israel, to restore or indemnify property destroyed in the hostilities. So much for the charges of official persecution. Israel's record speaks for itself and needs no defending. The Arabs are silent concerning the 700,000 Jews hounded in Arab lands, driven from their homes, thrown in jail, maltreated, hanged. Fortunately, many of these have found their way to Israel – though not all, as the executions in Baghdad attest.

And now to the accusations that Jews committed atrocities during the War of Independence.

Arab atrocities against Jews extend back to 1921. They include massacres, looting, crimes of all description. I don't invoke these to excuse or justify any violence committed by our people. All excesses are unjustifiable and, in my opinion, less excusable when committed by Jews than by anyone else because of our humanist traditions. Nevertheless, the Arab attitude towards us provoked a climate of tension that undoubtedly gave rise to hysterical reactions by individuals on both sides.

During the War of Independence our troops had to enter some Arab villages and hunt for munitions' stocks and armaments. That I consider a legitimate action, unpleasant to all concerned but legitimate.

However, it would be dishonest and foolish not to admit that a few, a very few criminal acts were committed during the first months of the war by some of the Jewish irregular forces who believed that Jewish terrorism was the only answer to the Arab terrorism that was perpetually plaguing our settlements and to the menace of an overwhelming enemy. These irregulars also practised such tactics against the British. They blew up the lobby of the King David Hotel in Jerusalem, where the British had their staff headquarters, and they have been accused of shooting Arab civilians in the village of Deir Yassin a few miles from Jerusalem. About two hundred unarmed persons are believed to have died in that raid carried out by members of Irgun.

Historical records indicate that the official government and the Jewish Agency, which acted as a pre-government and of which I was head, severely condemned the above acts as they condemned all terrorist initiatives in general. We were the first to publicize these actions and denounce them. I personally worked with all my strength to eliminate private armies, terrorists and other fanatic elements, to bring order and discipline to our military activities. This was achieved in record time for so beleaguered a state as ours. And I think that extremist actions committed by Jews were minimal, given constant Arab provocation and the desperate nature of the struggle both of which factors contributed to the situation's tenseness.

There is never an excuse for inhumanity. Yet all people are prone to hysteria under certain circumstances. I reproach the Arabs with many things but I do not hold against the Moslem population of this area as a whole the horrible lynching of seventy-seven Israeli doctors, nurses and students burned alive at this time on Mount Scopus. This was a mob action provoked by terror. The fact of this atrocity doesn't mitigate Deir Yassin or any other criminality on the part of Jewish elements. War calls up the worst in men as it also calls up the best. I can only reiterate that the government of Israel and the Jewish Agency before it, clamped down hard on all abuses. Once the

State was underway we ensured that they no longer occurred. Given the circumstances and the provocations of long-term Arab brutality towards the Jews, there were very few excesses indeed.

As for the present condition of Israel's Arab population – that population is quite aware today that economically its position is far superior to that of any other Arab group, including the Lebanese. Are our Arab citizens friendly towards us? I cannot say because one is in no position to ascertain their innermost thoughts. But they do have democratic representation, some of them do volunteer for service in our Forces and they have no material cause for hating us.

Far from practising genocide, we have done all in our power to raise the living standards of those Arabs who came under our jurisdiction subsequent to the Six Day War. It becomes less and less certain with each passing day that this population is interested in carrying on active war against us. We have left their local governments intact whenever possible; we have listened to their complaints and helped them to the best of our ability. They have free access to their shrines and are able to maintain their integrity as Moslems while obeying the very minimal regulations that we must impose upon them. As a captive population, they have had favoured treatment. Especially when one thinks what an Arab victory would mean to a Jewish population given the bloodthirsty Islamic concepts of celebrating triumphs.

I think the scope of free speech and press given to this Arab population by the Israeli authorities is truly remarkable, a model for all to learn from. I think it equally striking that not a single Arab terrorist has been executed by Israel for wanton, gratuitous acts of destruction that have claimed Israeli lives. We can take pride in the maturity, good sense and good will we have displayed in our relations with these people.

General Moshe Dayan tells a story of how he once consulted the Arab Mayor of Nablus, a city on the West Bank of the river Jordan that was captured by us in June 1967. The

Mayor is an Arab and frankly hostile to Israel. He is allowed to
express that hostility whenever he feels like it and to anyone he
can buttonhole, including the population at large and the
foreign press. He is not allowed to go out and blow up super-
markets or cinemas. But in his words and in his writings
he can rant and rave as much as his heart desires. And he is well
aware of it as the following story shows.

Dayan went to see him on an official visit to ask him what he
required for his administration. He didn't hesitate to ask for a
long list of items and services including a direct telephone line
to Tel Aviv. 'You understand, General, that it is impossible for
us to do business efficiently if we don't have a direct telephone
service to the coast,' said the Mayor. 'At present the system is
very cumbersome and involves going through the telephone
central in Jerusalem.' Dayan agreed and promised to see to the
installation of new telephone lines within the week (try getting such service in a European country, by the way!). Then
the two men had tea and Dayan asked politely: 'Mr Mayor,
how many times a day do you pray?' The Mayor said he
prayed the regulation number of Moslem occasions during the
day. 'Well,' said Dayan, 'how many times a day would you
pray if you could destroy Israel?' And the Mayor answered:
'For that, I would pray all day long.' The two men laughed,
shook hands and as Dayan left the Mayor reminded him about
the telephones to Tel Aviv. 'Just think,' Dayan said later, 'here
I am worrying about telephones for a man who prays for my
destruction!' And that sums up our relations with our new
Arab population. We give them such commodities as telephones; they call on Allah to annihilate us.

And yet, that population is growing increasingly less hostile. We are having our troubles with terrorism and sabotage
these days. But the instigators of these acts come from outside.
The Arabs here are living too well to participate actively in
these anti-social aggressions whose bad effects on them are felt
immediately by the security measures we are forced to take.
Given time, the Moslems under Israeli authority will become

less and less enthusiastic about the so-called Palestinian nationalists and ever more desirous of profiting from peaceful
relations with us. Again, the advent of new generations will
help this process along.

Already, Sabras are closer to the Arabs than were their
immigrant predecessors. Many of the former speak Arabic.
Most of my contemporaries didn't find it necessary to do so.
I myself can read Arabic through my knowledge of Turkish –
and of Hebrew. I spent three years learning Turkish during
my early days here. This turned out a waste of time since
Turkey's dominion over the territory we wanted to make
into Israel rapidly ended. But the language is about sixty
per cent Arabic so in that way it was useful for me to have
acquired it.

Today, I read in Arabic and especially in the Koran. I am
always surprised at the numbers of words resembling Hebrew.
These often have different meanings in the two tongues but as
words they are the same with the same origins.

This raises another important point militating for peace and
answering Arab charges that we are interlopers. Of course, we
are not! Ethnically we belong here. Jews and Arabs are
Semitic peoples and their natural habitat is the Middle East.
There is less difference between our peoples than between
Welsh and English, or Brittany French, who are Celts, and
Southern French who are Latins. Arabs and Jews belong
together as Swedes and Norwegians go together. Norway and
Sweden manage to live side by side in perfect accord yet each
enjoys its own autonomy. This is all we want for Israel. Let me
add that Norway and Sweden know how to co-operate for
their mutual economic and political benefit. This, too, could
happen here to the profit of all concerned.

It might not please the Russians, but the day the Middle
East evolves a Common Market this whole area could achieve
true economic independence. And Israel has a considerable
contribution to make towards such an initiative. Perhaps it is
futile to dwell on what might be were not things as they pre-

sently are. But if we can impress upon our neighbours what riches they have to gain from making peace with us, the generations of the future may see the light.

To the Jews, however, I have a different message, almost an opposite one since it is couched in more urgent terms. Israel can accomplish great things but it needs manpower. It is pleasant to talk of peace but the fact remains that we are at war. And though we can hope for a happy resolution some day, the possibility that we may have to fight another war like the action of June 1967, or maybe several such wars, is always present. That Israel will win these conflicts I have no doubt. At least not for now. What may happen in twenty years, I cannot say. But in the next five years we are sure to remain victorious, unless of course the Russians declare war on us. I don't think this is likely, but who can be sure?

The point is, however, that the Arabs can be defeated a hundred times and if they win the hundred and first time, that is the end for us! This is a truth our people don't realize sufficiently – I am speaking of Jews all over the world. When we defeat the Arabs it is not a true defeat for them because they can always tell themselves that victory will come in the last battle. If the Jews would realize this, they would come. Not merely for the defensive purpose of helping us keep Israel secure, but also for the positive reason that the key to this country's redemption lies in its total development, especially as carried on in the southern wastes. And the Jews of the world must realize that under the assimilationist pressures now at work in the Diaspora, their existence is seriously compromised without Israel's presence. I think that if the Jews would realize these things, and also realize that the Arabs too are modernizing, improving, becoming more formidable as an enemy, then they would come; the best of them would come.

If another two or three million immigrants would settle here, if for the time being we could count on two million more to give us a total Jewish population of four and a half million, then I would no longer fear for Israel's future.

10·Amsagolah

Moses told the Jews that they had a mission on earth. In his con-
clusion, Ben-Gurion indicates the significance of this mission and
defines the moral responsibility it implies.

WE have discussed the early history of the Jewish State and my personal reminiscences of the pioneering life. We have looked at some of its institutions, notably our Defence Forces and reviewed a few of our current problems and perspectives. In ending, however, I should like to follow the advice that Plato gives in his *Republic* to view what one has seen in close-up from afar. Let us examine from a distance, in general terms, what we can discern as the basic meaning of Israel's existence and the fundamental mission of the Jewish people here after so long an absence.

I can think of no better source for this purpose than the earlier sections of Torah. They contain the seed of that which results in our presence here today, from the secular as well as the religious viewpoint. What is Israel? It is two things: an Ark and a Covenant; in other words a refuge and a dynamic. I think the dynamic, the Covenant, takes precedence over the concept of refuge. A great number of Jews, I am sure, agree with me.

There are some who see Israel's importance primarily as an Ark, a place where the persecuted can go or hope to go. In Russia today, the harassed Jew looks secretly towards Israel. In

Poland, Jews who only a few months ago could bear to live under that country's regime have suddenly been forced out by recent anti-Semitic manifestations. Jewish intellectuals who had tolerated every sort of injustice perpetrated on the population of Poland in the name of Stalinism, Khruschevism, Brezhnevism, and who lost no occasion to denounce Israel as a wicked, capitalistic machination, have arrived here of late demanding asylum. We have given it to them because we are, effectively, an Ark. They are Jews no matter what their past. And they are entitled to be in Israel. Let us hope they have learned a lesson!

An Ark, however, is passive. We are a busy, forward-looking nation with much more work to accomplish. Israel cannot just be a refuge. If it is to survive as a valid nation it has to be much, much more.

For most Jews, Israel is Zion. Zion has special meaning for our people everywhere. Ultimately, it is the meaning of home. Israel is the Jewish home. As such it is a haven. But it is also a functioning enterprise with a future to fulfil and to look forward to.

And our mission here? What have the Jewish people to accomplish in Israel?

About 3,300 years ago there lived a Jew, the greatest Jew of all, who defined the mission of his people here. His definition is as good now as when he formulated it. I refer, of course, to Moshe. In English he is called Moses but that spoils the sound so I shall use the original Hebrew. The story of Moshe, then, is a mine of information about the Jews and the attitudes they have preserved – and that have preserved them – through the millennia.

Moshe starts life ignorant of his Jewish identity. Circumstance makes him an assimilationist, an Egyptian gentleman at a time when Jews are being persecuted as slaves. One day, however, he sees Egyptian soldiers killing a defenceless Jewish man. Something, he knows not what, pushes him to intervene. Moshe thus begins adulthood marked by that activist conscience we have noted as a Jewish characteristic.

A very simple tale this, yet it makes the point that a Jew is a Jew. We are not a people who assimilate easily. That, of course, is why we still exist. Through four thousand years there have always been such as Moshe to stand up and be counted as men and as Jews.

After fleeing to exile and following his first contact with God in the Burning Bush, Moshe returns to Egypt to lead his people to freedom. He takes them to the desert on the way to the Promised Land. The Children of Israel wander in the wilderness that I can see out of my window at Sde Boker. They live this life for forty years, an act of purification and reaffirmation of Judaism which Moshe imposes upon them in the name of the Lord, as a pre-requisite to penetrating the land they will make their own. One can see how secular and religious explanations coincide. During those forty years, the Canaanite strongholds were too well fortified to allow the Israelites access into the more fertile area near the Mediterranean. But as the Canaanites sank into corruption and weakness, the Israelites by their nomadic frugality were gaining strength and new faith both in their God and in themselves. On the eve of battle they affirm their belief in the Almighty to Joshua who only after hearing their allegiance leads them to the conquest of Canaan.

Moshe did not live to set foot in the Promised Land. But he gave the Jews the basic elements for their unique moral code that provides the key to their enduring significance to world history and civilization. That code is the Ten Commandments as coupled to Moshe's other special message that a man must love his neighbour as himself. Moshe left a vision of love and of union between men. That was his greatest contribution.

To the Jews he said something more. He said to them: 'You are a nation of God.' He added: 'This means you must be Amsagolah.'

I have tried to find an adequate translation for the word 'Amsagolah' in any of several languages. After consulting a dozen different dictionaries, I have had to give up hope of hitting on an exact equivalent to this Hebrew expression. Even in Greek there is no correct translation. I looked at the Greek first since this was the foreign tongue into which the Bible was originally rendered from the Jewish texts. In Latin I could find no really telling word or phrase for Amsagolah, nor in any modern language such as French, German, Russian or English. Amsagolah doesn't mean 'special' or 'superior'. It has the connotation of 'unique' and also one of its meanings might be expressed by the phrase 'higher virtues'. But these I fear are only partial implications. We might say that Moshe's message from God could thus be summed up: 'The Jews must be a unique nation in that they should embody the higher virtues.' In other words, the uniqueness of the Jews is not that they consider themselves to be singled out for special status by God, to be his favoured creatures or his super-race. It doesn't mean that like Moslems they can look forward to being the elect of Paradise. Rather Amsagolah implies an extra burden, an added responsibility to perform with a virtue born of conscience and to listen to what Elijah later called 'the still, small voice'.

The Jews took Moshe's uncompromising message to heart. Even today we are a compulsive people and our strong sense of conscience is evident in our collective as well as our individual personalities. In the majority of Jews one finds something pushing from within to accomplish more, to do better, to follow a path of active virtue that doesn't correspond to the Christian avoidance of damnation. The Jews have little sense of a Hell waiting under their feet. Their hell is more a personal dissatisfaction born of mediocrity. I think this is why Jews are always bothering themselves, and others, with trying to discern general, ultimate principles from particular things. It is their biggest fault and greatest blessing. But whatever the outcome of these compulsions, their origins undoubtedly lie in an innate Judaic awareness of Amsagolah and its demands upon the conscience.

So Moshe told us we must be Amsagolah and this was the

ideal given to our people at the beginning of our permanent settlement in Israel. We know from the Bible that often they fell far short of this goal, and indeed were as a nation no better than their neighbours. Yet in every generation there were men who asked questions, who struggled to attain a higher virtue and who implanted the message of Amsagolah in their people. Judges, Prophets, Sages all demanded the spiritual elevation of the House of Israel. None preached war, power politics, master-race theories. They weren't concerned with outsiders but with the Jewish conscience *vis-à-vis* itself. They demanded of the Jews to look inward to struggle towards righteousness and to fight against evil. Israel was to spread morality throughout the universe. It was to do so not by conquest but by example. Thus would other nations learn from Israel's ways and walk in the footsteps of the Bible.

And so they have. The wise men were right. With some modification, Islam and Christianity adopted many basic ideas from the Jews. I think that today we must heed these ancient teachers again. By cultivating Amsagolah and all it implies we shall find the strength to build this land as we must. In time, the nations around us will learn from our ways and extend the hand of peace.

The message of Moshe and Judaism's monotheistic belief are two of the pillars on which the Jewish faith has rested through time. The third pillar is the ideal of Israel and the mingling of Jewish philosophy with national history. The other deities contemporary to the Lord of Abraham and Moshe are long dead, as are the civilizations that invented them. The Jews live on. The three Judaic pillars are responsible for our survival.

Moshe's Amsagolah gave the Jewish people something to struggle towards. They have never attained it; perhaps it is unattainable in its totality. Yet I think the goal itself produced such humanistic inspirations as the kibbutz idea, an institution at once very Jewish, very Israeli but also very adaptable to universal requirements. Kibbutzim are now evolving in Japan and elsewhere. I once asked the Russian ambassador – in the days when we had Russian ambassadors – whether there were kibbutzim in the Soviet Union. 'No,' he said. 'Perhaps in forty or fifty years we shall have them!'

I have always been very concerned, secularist though I am, with this country's spiritual state. As soon after Independence as feasible, I called together our leading intellectuals including such thinkers as Martin Buber and the philosopher Hugo Bergmann. I said to them: 'Up to now we have been at war which is against all our aims and hopes for Israel. We still have the threat of war to contend with as well as incalculable numbers of material problems. I know the Marxists would say only material problems count. But I am mindful of the Talmud which tells us that "where there is no bread there is no Torah but also where there is no Torah there is no bread." And I asked them to define spiritual aims for Israel's development which we should endeavour to strive for concurrently with our effort in matters of practical necessity. Those conferences were in part responsible for the great emphasis we immediately put on education, despite the drain on the budget this implied for a State surrounded by enemy armies.

Words without deeds are nothing. This I learned in the Bible and for myself from the moment I set foot in this land. Telling people: 'You must be good. You must help others,' accomplishes little. One must show the way by example. That is why I live at Sde Boker, to underline to all who come in contact with me the importance of this Negev area to our future. One must use words to communicate ideas and feelings. But words without the capacity to evoke deeds are meaningless.

Today I live alone here, and I work with words. I am writing, as I have said, the history of the modern Jewish State. I want the young people of Israel to realize how precious a heritage we of the older generations are delivering into their hands. They have both the privilege of carrying our work through to fuller fruition and the obligation to do so. They, too, are under the Jewish injunction to be an Amsagolah. The realization of this inherited burden is what I hope my book will contribute to.

You cannot reach for the higher virtue without being an idealist. The Jews are chronic idealists which makes me humbly glad to belong to this people and to have shared in their noble epic. In a time when their neighbours were sacrificing live children to the fires of the idol Moloch they had evolved their invisible God, a God who forbade human sacrifice and who imposed a law of love and respect for all beings and things of this earth. They codified this in the Bible and dreamt their dream of redemption in their land. Only a small part of this dream has ever come true and we have borne much suffering because of it. But the dream is there, the moral idea is there and as in the time of Moshe, the Jews must strive so long as they endure to be an Amsagolah. 'I the Lord have called thee in righteousness and have taken hold of thy hand and kept thee and set thee for a Covenant of the people, for a light unto the nations.' (Isaiah 42–6).

CHRONOLOGY

16 October 1886

David Gryn is born in Plonsk, a market town in northern
Poland, then under Russian Tsarist rule. He is the fourth
child of Avigdor Gryn, a lawyer, and Sheindal Friedman
Gryn. The family lives in the Jewish community of Plonsk
which occupies the city's central residential quarter and
numbers about five thousand.

1889

One of David Gryn's earliest memories is of his grandfather
teaching him Hebrew at the age of three. The boy is also
very attached to his mother who dies when he is ten. His
father is a 'Lover of Zion', later an ardent Zionist, also a
freethinker. The boy David is brought up on Zionism,
reveres Theodor Herzl, founder of the international Zionist
movement, as a near-Messiah for his leadership in the cause
of actively creating a Jewish homeland.

1886–1904

Zionism spreads through the Jewish communities of Eastern
Europe and especially inspires the youth.

Circa 1900

David Gryn and his contemporaries organize the Ezra
Society to support Zionism and the socialist pioneering ideal
in Palestine. Ezra members teach Hebrew to the entire
Plonsk community (which commonly speaks Yiddish and
Russian, considering Hebrew as a literary and scholarly
'dead' language).

1904–6

David Gryn and his friends are shocked into action by the
proposal, championed by some Zionists, to accept a British
offer of territory in Uganda for the Jewish National Home.
In protest, Gryn's older friend, Shlomo Zemach, leaves for
Palestine.

August 1906

David Gryn goes to Palestine.

1906–8

Young Gryn works as a farm labourer in the various Jewish
settlements of central Palestine. He suffers from malaria.
Labour is scarce and in his weakened condition he has great
difficulty in finding enough work to keep from starving. A
doctor tells him that if he stays in Palestine, the malaria will
surely kill him. Nevertheless, he remains and despite the
doctor's prediction slowly regains strength.

1908–10

David Gryn joins a group of pioneers in the Galilee. They prepare swamps and rocky plains for cultivation by Jewish settlers. Land is being bought in the North by the Jewish National Fund. Gryn meets Itzhak Ben-Zvi, the future State of Israel's second President. Ben-Zvi is one of the few immigrants speaking Hebrew. Both he and Gryn militate for the idea that creating a Jewish homeland will require the re-establishment of Hebrew as the Jewish language.

This is the era when the first kibbutzim are organized by Galilee pioneers. Gryn does not join a kibbutz but attaches himself to a pioneer camp at Sejera. The Jewish settlements and camps are raided by Arab bandits. Gryn and his companions decide to create a self-defence force called Hashomer or 'The Watchmen'. This is the beginning of Jewish–Arab friction in Palestine. Hashomer also marks the beginning of what will one day become a Jewish army.

1910

Gryn abandons pioneering for politics. With Ben-Zvi, he becomes a journalist in Jerusalem. They are members of the socialist Poale Zion (Workers of Zion) Party. Gryn Hebraicizes his family name to Ben-Gurion in honour of a former David Ben-Gurion who died with the last defenders of Jerusalem in 70 C.E. The date marks the Roman capture of the city and the exile of the Jewish people from nationhood, a period lasting 1,878 years until the founding of the State of Israel in 1948.

1912

Ben-Gurion and his associates decide that to militate

effectively for Jewish immigration and autonomy in Palestine they must work within the framework of the Turkish Empire. The Empire itself is in upheaval, with wave after wave of young officers replacing previous leaders in a series of military takeovers. Each new group speaks of liberty and solicits the support of minorities within the Empire's territories. Ben-Gurion feels the Jews' best hope for a permanent community in Palestine is to come to an agreement with the Turks whereby a certain measure of autonomy will be granted them in return for their loyalty. He decides to militate from within the Turkish political and social system. He sports Turkish dress and a moustache, journeys to Constantinople and enrols as a law student at the University with the intention of entering politics upon graduation.

1914–15

The First World War destroys all such illusions. Ben-Gurion and Ben-Zvi, who had also gone to Constantinople, hastily return to Jerusalem where they are confronted with a general exodus of Jews fleeing in panic to Egypt. Chaim Weizmann in London, Joseph Trumpeldor and Vladimir Jabotinsky in Egypt, call upon the Jews to support the Allies. For Ben-Gurion and Ben-Zvi the Allies mean Russia which in turn calls up memories of the Tsar and anti-Semitic persecution. So they do not heed this call but continue to campaign in Palestine for immigration and integration into the Turkish Empire.

They work to organize Hashomer into a general Jewish militia for the defence of Palestine and the protection of what the Jews already have in the country.

March 1915

In Egypt, the former Tsarist officer and Zionist, Joseph Trumpeldor, organizes a Zionist Muleteer Corps to fight for the British, with the hope that the latter will take up the cause of a Jewish homeland in Palestine (the British have already indicated their awareness of the Jewish need for a national home by offering Uganda in the early part of the century). Volunteers for the Trumpeldor corps leave Palestine for Alexandria where it is assembling. Ben-Gurion and Ben-Zvi oppose this initiative on grounds that the Turks may carry out reprisals against the Jews who stay in Palestine and because they consider direct, local defence of Jewish property more important to the Zionist cause.

Late Summer 1915

The Turks discover a Hashomer arms cache and decide the Jews might be a fifth column working for the British. They arrest many Jews and expel them from the country. Ben-Gurion and Ben-Zvi are among the first to suffer expulsion and they sail to the United States.

Autumn 1915

Ben-Gurion and Ben-Zvi arrive in New York. They have discarded all hope of Turkish support for Zionism and are ready to enlist the aid of the British. They recruit for a Jewish Legion which Vladimir Jabotinsky, now in London, is attempting to organize within the British Army. They also establish the Hechalutz ('Pioneer') movement in the United States. The aim of this movement is to encourage the emigration of young people who will work as pioneers in Palestine.

2 November 1917

The Balfour Declaration announces that the British
government is ready to support the establishment in Palestine
of a national home for the Jewish people. The declaration
exceeds even the most optimistic hopes of the Zionists. It is
a diplomatic triumph and one for the diplomatists – as
distinct from the immigrants to Palestine – of the Zionist
Movement. Ben-Gurion, sounding a cautionary note typical
of his pioneer viewpoint, writes at the time: 'Britain has
made a magnificent gesture; she has recognized our
existence as a nation and has acknowledged our right to the
country. But only the Hebrew people can transform this
right into tangible fact; only they, with body and soul, with
their strength and capital, can build their National Home
and bring about their national redemption.'

5 December 1917

David Ben-Gurion marries Pauline Munweiss in New York.
She is known ever afterwards as 'Paula' to the entire Zionist
Movement.

Early 1918

Jabotinsky finally succeeds in establishing a Jewish Legion
within the British Army. It is composed of regular British
units whose uniforms bear an identifying Shield of David.
Ben-Gurion joins one of these units in Canada, the 39th
Battalion of the Royal Fusiliers.

June 1918

Jabotinsky's Legion sees action in Palestine.

Autumn 1918

Ben-Gurion's battalion sails for the Middle East but doesn't arrive until the fighting there has ended.

Late 1918

The Balfour Declaration is formally approved by the United States, France and most significantly of all, in the name of the Arab peoples through a special treaty of friendship drawn up by T. E. Lawrence (of Arabia) and signed by both Weizmann and Prince Feisal, later King Feisal I, of Iraq.

1919–20

Ben-Gurion's first child, a girl with the Hebrew name of Geula, meaning 'redemption', is born. Now that he is back in Palestine, Ben-Gurion enters politics once more by launching a campaign for workers' unity. The Jewish settlements in the country are in a sad state and much of the work accomplished over fifty years is in ruins. Nevertheless, immigration increases and Ben-Gurion struggles to create a cohesive organization among Palestine's Jews and especially among the workers and pioneers. This culminates in the founding of the Histadruth or Confederation of Labour. Its aims are to mobilize all pioneers, farmers and workers for a future Jewish State under the slogan: 'We must make a nation of the class we represent.' Histadruth constitutes the only large-scale political body in Palestine.

1920

Ben-Gurion becomes General-Secretary of the Histadruth

which numbers 4,443 members. At this time, the population of Palestine is roughly 10,000 Jews and 800,000 Arabs. Several million Jews belong to Zionist organizations as grouped in a World Federation.

1920–22

These are years of growing tension, violence, troubles of many varieties. As early as 1920, hostility breaks out between Arabs and Jews. Joseph Trumpeldor, Zionism's greatest military hero, is shot down by Arabs in the Galilee. Inflamed by the religious leader, Hadj Amin el Husseini, the Arabs kill Jews in acts of scattered violence. The latter respond by organizing a clandestine defence force (the British at this time refuse to countenance an official Jewish defence system) which they call Haganah (Defence). This groups all the Hashomer units and also links up to the Histadruth.

1922

The San Remo Conference of the League of Nations approves the British Mandate over Palestine and the creation of a Jewish National Home under the terms of the Balfour Declaration. But in a move to appease the Arabs, Britain issues a White Paper, drawn up by Winston Churchill, excluding all areas east of the Jordan river from the Mandate and there establishing an artificial state called Transjordan with its capital in the village of Amman.

1922–5

Ben-Gurion militates for socialism in the Jewish communities of Palestine, and for the employment of Jewish labour there.

Immigration increases rapidly from the war-torn and disrupted lands of Europe. The number of immigrants becomes a near-flood after the United States establishes a quota system which effectively bars masses of Eastern Europeans from its territory.

The problem now becomes not so much to encourage immigration but to provide facilities and work for those who do arrive. Unemployment increases alarmingly and so does the rate of immigrants who leave the country unable to find a place for themselves. Ben-Gurion journeys to Europe to mobilize the resources of the international Zionist Movement in favour of Palestine's immigrant population.

A son, Amos, is born to the Ben-Gurion family at this time.

1925

Ben-Gurion's aged father, Avigdor Gryn, arrives from Plonsk, Poland. The Ben-Gurions' third and last child, a daughter named Renana, is born. All of the Gryn family is now in Palestine except for a niece who remains in Plonsk. She and her two children go to the gas chamber at Auschwitz.

1925–7

Ben-Gurion represents the Palestine workers in the Zionist movement of Europe where he militates for financial support of immigrants and the creation of job and pioneering possibilities. In Jerusalem, he lives in poverty, with barely enough money to keep his family going.

His relations with the Zionist delegates and with the British grow increasingly stormy. He reproaches the Zionists with being armchair pioneers having too little

contact with and sensitivity towards the immigrants who
are doing the actual work of building the country. He is
impatient with increasing British reserve towards the Jews
in the light of Arab hostility. He also clashes with other
Palestinian Jewish groups, notably the Revisionists under
Jabotinsky, who fear Histadruth's power and one-class
outlook. The Revisionists call Histadruth a 'state within a
state'.

1927–30

Largely owing to the efforts of Ben-Gurion, various political
factions in Palestine coalesce with Histadruth to form
MAPAI or The Workers' United Party. But conditions in
the country are rapidly going from bad to worse.
Unemployment is on the rise as is friction between Arabs
and Jews, exacerbated by Hadj Amin el-Husseini who has
been appointed Mufti of Jerusalem by British High
Commissioner Sir Herbert Samuel. Husseini as Mufti is
administrative head of the Moslem religious community in
Palestine. He is a fanatic and groups a violent following
under the slogan 'Death to the Jews'. Lord Samuel, a Jew
himself, has for that very reason favoured Husseini's
appointment as an indication of impartiality. The hope was
to appease this potential troublemaker by giving him the
highest office he could aspire to in Palestine. But as Mufti,
Husseini becomes an ever more dangerous source of
discontent. He has visions of restoring the Caliphate and
expelling all non-Arab elements from the country. He
instigates a massacre of Jews in Jerusalem by spreading the
rumour that they plan to rebuild their ruined Temple on the
site of the Mosque of Omar (itself constructed partially on
the Temple site). Husseini is also directly responsible for
provoking Arab–Jewish friction that culminates on 23
August 1929 in an Arab invasion of the Jewish areas of

Jerusalem with a general attack on the population. This is echoed by riots in Hebron, Jaffa, Safed. At least 140 Jews are killed and thousands injured. British intervention comes too late and is largely ineffectual.

1930–36

The rise of Fascism in Europe. Arab hostility to the Jews continues to be fanned by the Mufti who soon establishes relations with the new Nazi regime in Germany. In 1936 the Arabs murder more Jews. Leaders of the Jewish communities can barely restrain the young people in Haganah from fighting back and thus starting a civil war. Arab dockworkers in Jaffa stage a general strike and the Mufti demands that the British stop Jewish immigration and prohibit the Jews from buying further land in Palestine. He calls for Arab autonomy and a totally Arab government for the country. Moshe Sharett, Israel's second Prime Minister-to-be, in a letter to the London *Times* on behalf of the MAPAI Party, states categorically: 'If the demands of the Palestinian Arabs are met by Great Britain, this would mean the end of the Jewish people's hopes of taking root as a nation in their homeland.' The Zionist Committee is not convinced of this and Dr Weizmann even suggests that as a means of restoring peace a temporary halt be put on Jewish immigration. Ben-Gurion in London heads off this proposal before it is put to the British.

1936

Because of continual difficulties with Arab dockworkers in Jaffa, the Jewish pioneers decide to create their own outlet to the sea. They choose a site as near as possible to the standard shipping lanes, at Tel Aviv. In record time they

build a settlement complete with port facilities. Thus is born
what today is Israel's largest city.

July 1937

In the latter part of the previous year Britain had named a
Commission under Lord Peel to study the Palestine problem.
In July 1937 the Peel Commission publishes its report
recommending the division of the country into three parts:
Jewish, Arab and British. According to this plan, the Jews
should establish a wholly autonomous and independent
state in the Galilee and Valley of Jezreel, an area comprising
about one-fifth of Western Palestine. The Arabs would get
almost the entire remainder of the country which would be
incorporated into the newly created state of Transjordan
owing its existence to the Churchill White Paper of 1922.
The British would keep Jerusalem, Nazareth and a corridor
to the Mediterranean that includes the port of Haifa.

MAPAI, Histadruth and the Zionist Movement are all
ready and delighted to accept the Commission's proposal on
the grounds that, small as the designated Jewish territory is,
it nevertheless constitutes a basis for the formation of a
Jewish State in Palestine. The 'Revisionist' group under
Jabotinsky's leadership protests that this would give the Jews
much less than the promises implied by the Balfour
Declaration.

1939

The Peel Commission's findings and the problem of a
Jewish state become academic with the publication of a new
British White Paper drawn up by Malcolm MacDonald
under the aegis of Foreign Secretary Lord Halifax, in the
Neville Chamberlain government. Despite all previous

recommendations and declarations, this White Paper fixes a Jewish immigration quota for Palestine and assigns a schedule for the country's independence under Arab rule. The quota allows the Jews to bring in a mere 75,000 more persons over a five year period after which all immigration is to cease. In ten years, the British will pull out leaving the Arabs in control and the Jews as a weak minority in the country.

Meanwhile, as war looms and the 'Final Solution' begins grinding the Jewish population of Europe to oblivion, Ben-Gurion makes his famous statement of the Jews' double battle: 'We shall fight the war as if there were no White Paper,' he declares, 'and the White Paper as if there were no war!'

1940

Churchill replaces Chamberlain and Lord Lloyd, Lord Halifax. Weizmann and Ben-Gurion call for a new Jewish legion. Ben-Gurion is at this time Chairman of the Jewish Agency.

May 1942

A Congress Extraordinary organized by the American Committee for Zionist Affairs with Ben-Gurion as prime-mover calls for defiance of the British immigration embargo, demands a Jewish state and undertakes to finance resistance to all attempts to impede immigration and the National Home in Palestine.

1944

A Jewish Brigade, attached to the British Army, is finally

formed. It participates in the invasion of Sicily and Italy,
then fights its way across the Continent of Europe from
Holland to Berlin.

1945

Ben-Gurion tours the concentration camps and declares:
'During these six years of war, we never forgot you for a
single day. We have been working to build up our land so
that you may come there to live as decent human beings
again among your own people and where you will not fear
again.'

1945–7

Despite Ben-Gurion's words, the British Labour Government
vigorously enforces the 1939 embargo on Jewish immigration
to Palestine. Foreign Secretary Ernest Bevin declares total
restriction of Jewish immigration, ignoring the fact that a
million or so homeless Jews are flooding the displaced
persons camps of central Europe. The Zionists make good
their intention to fight the 1939 White Paper and its
aftermath. They organize massive illegal immigration,
leading to skirmishes with the British and worldwide
concern with the problem, generated by such incidents as
the fate of the SS *Exodus*. This is a barely seaworthy vessel,
crowded to the gunwhales with Jewish immigrants from the
European camps and forced to wander across the
Mediterranean while those aboard starve rather
than accept internment and deportation back to
Germany, Austria, Poland, the scene of the holocaust,
by the British.

1947

A crop of Jewish private armies spring up clandestinely in
Palestine. Each has its own particular political orientation.
Often they are as busy fighting each other as they are
fighting their common foes. The purpose of these groups is
to wage active war on the Arabs (as a counter to continual
harassment of Jewish communities) and show hostility to
the British who are deeply resented because of their anti-
immigration policy and for general attitudes that appear to
favour the Arab cause. Irgun and the Stern organization are
the best known of the private Jewish armies. Haganah, later
to become the official Army of Israel, gathers weapons in
secret, trains for combat but abstains from acts of aggression.
Under its aegis, however, kibbutz members train in the
special attack corps called Palmach or 'The Striking Force'.
This too holds back from actual combat except in local
defence against Arabs.

Britain suddenly estimates that Palestine is not worth the
expense and effort required to keep the peace between
Arabs and Jews. It wishes to end the bad international
publicity generated by the immigration policy. So it appeals
to the United Nations to take over the problem. The UN
establishes yet another Commission to study Palestine. This
Commission splits into a majority and minority faction with
the UN opting for the majority recommendations, largely
inspired by the Peel Commission findings of a decade earlier.
The UN decides that:

i)   Britain is to leave Palestine and end its Mandate no
later than 1 August 1948.

ii)   A small area of Palestine including a northern coastal
section, the Galilee and Valley of Jezreel, some frontage
along the Dead Sea and a non-contiguous territory in
the Negev to go to the Jews as an independent state.

iii) The rest of the territory, a much larger area, to go to the Palestinian Arabs and also be considered an independent state.

iv) Jerusalem to be an independent city under an autonomous government comprising both Arab and Jewish representatives and undertaking to guarantee religious freedom with unrestricted access to all shrines and places of worship. The Jewish and Arab populations are to live there freely under international charter and have equal representation in the municipal authority.

1947

The Jews accept the UN ruling. The Arabs reject it. They declare they will fight for control of all Palestine including Jerusalem. The Palestinian Arabs contract an alliance with Egypt, Syria, Lebanon, and Transjordan for the destruction of the proposed Jewish state and the control of Jerusalem.

1948

Before the British Mandate ends, the Arabs attack and seize control of the single road leading from Jerusalem to the sea. Their intention is to starve out the city's Jewish population which is concentrated mainly in what is now West Jerusalem, with a small enclave in the eastern sector, the most ancient quarter where the ruined wall of the Temple stands. The Arabs also seize the city's water reservoirs shutting down the supply to West Jerusalem. The Jewish population of Jerusalem must act quickly or capitulate to Arab rule.

Palmach, the attack unit of Haganah, gathers a heterogeneous collection of vehicles held together with baling wire and ingenuity. On Ben-Gurion's order (he has now become head of a 'shadow Cabinet' preparing for independence), Palmach fights its way up the narrow, twisting road in what stands as one of the most heroic exploits in four thousand years of Jewish history. Through ambush and constant attack by an enemy superior in numbers and equipment and, moreover, holding the higher ground, Palmach forces its way to Jerusalem. It enters the city, restores the food and water supply, saves the population. A monument to the saving of Jerusalem is constituted by the dozen wrecked, rusting vehicles that today line the road leading to the city.

14 May 1948

The British pull out ahead of schedule. Ben-Gurion reads the Proclamation of Independence of the State of Israel. Dr Weizmann becomes its first President, Ben-Gurion the first Prime Minister.

15 May 1948

At dawn, Egyptian aircraft bomb Tel Aviv. The Arab Legion under General Sir John Bagot Glubb (who as Glubb Pasha served as its head until his dismissal by King Hussein of Jordan in 1956) marches from Transjordan on Jerusalem after secret negotiations between Ben-Gurion and King Abdullah of Transjordan fail. The armies of Egypt, Syria, Lebanon and Iraq invade Jewish territory.

May–June 1948

The USSR and the United States, in that order, recognize the State of Israel.

Jerusalem is now a battlefield. Fierce combat occurs in the Old City. The Jews hang on for several days but are hopelessly outnumbered and out-equipped. They must retreat to the Western sector. The older half of Jerusalem, including the Temple site, is abandoned to the Arab Legion. The Arabs reduce Jewish monuments and synagogues to rubble.

Note: Throughout the 1948 war, the Arabs utilize modern British and American military equipment. The Jews rely on what they have gathered clandestinely from British Mandate Forces and on shipments from Czechoslovakia as well as on what they manage to make for themselves. In this they show considerable ingenuity.

June 1948

The Ben-Gurion government considers the time has come to consolidate all Jewish fighting units into a unified official Israel Army. The existence of private armies makes for military fragmentation, bad strategic co-ordination and lack of discipline. The government feels this is one of the reasons for the loss of Jerusalem's Old City. Ben-Gurion therefore establishes an official Army and demands that all fighting units swear an oath of allegiance to its command. He is defied by Irgun and other groups wishing to retain their independence. Public opinion in Israel is divided on the issue.

The UN uses its good offices to obtain a four week truce. Both sides promise not to add to their arms' stock during this period. Swedish Count Folke Bernadotte journeys to Jerusalem to try and negotiate an Arab–Jewish settlement. Despite the truce provisions, the Arabs are known to be gathering arms and supplies in Egypt, Syria, Iraq. In Israel, Irgun defies the Ben-Gurion government's scrupulous adherence to the arms' ban and attempts to land a large consignment of military equipment from Czechoslovakia.

This equipment was ordered and paid for before the truce and was already en route to Israel aboard the freighter SS *Altalena*. Irgun starts trans-shipping arms from the ship to an Israel beach. Ben-Gurion orders Army shore batteries to open fire. The freighter sinks. Irgun leader, Menahem Beigin, aboard the *Altalena* at the time, barely escapes. The incident almost sparks civil war among the Jews and generates much bitterness between Israeli political factions. Nevertheless, government policy prevails and Israel's fighting forces co-ordinate under Ben-Gurion's command.

July 1948

Count Bernadotte is assassinated in Jerusalem by Jewish extremists. Fighting resumes. The newly unified Israeli Army drives the Arabs out of Jewish territory and forces their retreat from a large sector of Palestine, thus linking the non-contiguous area of the Negev to the rest of the country and increasing the national domain by about one third.

1949

The Arab nations sign an Armistice with Israel giving the latter all the territory it has conquered from the Lebanese frontier in the North to the tip of the Negev in the South. Jerusalem remains divided in two, with the eastern sector going to the newly established Hashemite Kingdom of Jordan. The boundaries fixed at this time endure through many viscissitudes for nineteen years until the Six Day War in June 1967 extends the area of Israeli jurisdiction.

11 May 1949

Israel becomes a member of the United Nations.

1949–50

The beginning of a long era of relative peace in which there is no war but continual acts of terrorism on the part of Arabs, as well as almost daily frontier skirmishes. Jews begin to immigrate from everywhere, from India and the United States, Holland and Morocco, fulfilling Isaiah's words: 'I will bring thy seed from the east and gather thee from the west . . .' A most dramatic arrival is that of 45,000 Yemenite Jews who bear out a Biblical prediction that they shall return 'on the backs of eagles' by arriving aboard the aircraft of El Al, Israel's fledgling international airline.

Immigration, encouraged by the Law of Return providing that any Jew has the right to live in Israel and claim Israeli citizenship, brings the problem of integrating a diverse people from all cultures, classes and lands including many from the underdeveloped areas of North Africa and the Middle East. The Army becomes a leading educational institution teaching literacy in Hebrew and technical skills to the younger generation.

The State puts itself in order. Despite heavy military commitments, funds are budgeted for free public schooling, a large-scale housing programme for immigrants, and a modern civil administration. Israel develops more schools and universities, hospitals, museums, art galleries, newspapers, magazines and symphony orchestras *per capita* over the next decade than any other nation in the world. Funds to accomplish this come mainly from Diaspora-Zionist contributions, especially from the United States.

1951

Egypt seizes the Straits of Tiran at the entrance to the Gulf of Eilath. It blockades the port of Eilath, thus compromising plans for developing this port and cultivating the Negev.

For the next five years Israel suffers constantly from shipping blockades and the sabotage of road, railway and irrigation systems by armed Egyptian commandos infiltrating across the frontiers from special bases in the Sinai Peninsula and the Gaza Strip. Hundreds of Israelis are killed in skirmishes with these commandos and many thousands wounded.

7 January 1952

At Ben-Gurion's instigation, Israel accepts eight hundred million dollars' reparations from West Germany. The Ben-Gurion government is strongly criticized for taking money from the Jews' former persecutors. Ben-Gurion argues that Israel desperately needs the funds for its development and that the reparations are not in compensation for the holocaust itself but for damage to property suffered by European Jewry in the Second World War.

9 December 1952

Dr Chaim Weizmann, Israel's first President, dies. Ben-Gurion approaches Dr Albert Einstein in the United States to offer him the Presidency. Einstein refuses. Itzhak Ben-Zvi, Ben-Gurion's oldest living friend and associate, becomes President.

13 December 1953

Ben-Gurion leaves the government provisionally to join a pioneer kibbutz at Sde Boker in the Negev. He steps down as Prime Minister and is set to tending sheep. Moshe Sharett becomes Israel's second Prime Minister. Pinhas Lavon takes over Ben-Gurion's portfolio as Defence Minister.

1954

Col. Abdel Nasser comes to power in Egypt at the age of
thirty-six. Of Nasser Ben-Gurion has said: 'I am quite
certain that there would have been intellectual contact
between us had we ever met.' Several attempts are made by
Israel to negotiate such a meeting and Ben-Gurion declares
publicly: 'I am ready to meet with the Egyptian Prime
Minister or with any other Arab leader at any place and any
time in order to arrive at a peace settlement without any
prior conditions.' At the time of the Suez conflict he even
expresses willingness to journey to Cairo for negotiations
provided his safe conduct is assured. Marshal Tito of
Yugoslavia is approached as an intermediary. He declines.
Nasser comments: 'I would be ready to meet with Ben-
Gurion but I am afraid that then I would not be able to
return to Cairo. One hour after my return, I would be
assassinated! It's too risky.' And so the two Middle Eastern
leaders most capable of obtaining a peace settlement are
never to meet.

July 1954

The British announce their intention of departing from the
Suez Canal Zone. For Israel, this implies a direct threat to all
shipping bound for its ports. The British pullout results in
the Lavon Affair.

The Lavon Affair is Israel's first political scandal since
nationhood. Michael Bar-Zohar in his biography of Ben-
Gurion entitled *The Armed Prophet* has called it 'the most
disastrous and scandalous secret warfare episode ever known
in the Middle East'. Nine years later this scandal which
refused to die is instrumental in provoking Ben-Gurion's
final resignation from government.

The Affair begins when the Egyptians uncover an Israeli

Secret Service plot to start a wave of terrorism in Cairo and Alexandria that can be attributed to a local organization calling itself the Moslem Brotherhood. The idea is to prove the weakness and incapacity to govern of the Egyptian authorities and thus persuade the British to remain in the Suez Canal Zone. The plot is revealed by an Israeli double agent. Arrests are made and two men subsequently hanged.

The Israeli government is totally unaware of this plot. Subsequent investigation indicates the possible complicity of Defence Minister Lavon under whose nominal control the Secret Service operates and who is known for his belligerent attitude towards Egypt. Lavon denies all knowledge of the plot. An inquiry is held the results of which are inconclusive. Lavon is quietly pressured to resign from government.

21 February 1955

Ben-Gurion returns from retirement to take over the Defence portfolio from his fallen protégé. He is shaken by the scandal and feels that nothing short of a public judicial inquiry into its origins will rub out the taint of the affair and restore full confidence in the government. His colleagues in the Cabinet feel otherwise and are satisfied with the results of the informal secret inquiry and Lavon's resignation. Thus the matter rides for several years.

1955

Ben-Gurion embarks on a search for alliances for Israel. He attempts to interest the Americans in guaranteeing the country's security in return for strategic bases. At this time the United States is pursuing a policy of encirclement of the USSR and negotiations look fruitful. In the end, however,

the Americans refuse to commit themselves to a definite
guarantee of Israel's frontiers.

Meanwhile, with the departure of the British from Suez
the USSR suddenly shifts its Middle Eastern policy and
from enthusiastic support of Israel becomes the champion of
Arab nationalism. It begins furiously to equip the Egyptian
Army and rail against Israel as an imperialist and
'colonialist' power.

26 July 1956

Egypt nationalizes the Suez Canal, taking control away from
the British–French consortium that operates it. The move
aligns Israeli, British and French interests causing a strong
rapprochement between Israel and France which in the
years to come is to be the former's chief military supplier. In
return, the Israelis contribute heavily to the improvement
development of French military equipment. It is no
exaggeration to say that the success of the French Mystère
fighter plane series is directly due to design improvements
and changes developed by the Israelis in operations.

Throughout 1955 and 1956 there is continuous frontier
trouble between Israel and Egypt due to Egyptian
commandos operating in Israeli territory and training
former Palestinian Arabs who at this time form themselves
into a movement called the Palestine Liberation Front.

1956

Israel is increasingly desirous of controlling access to
Eilath through the Gulf of Aqaba and of ensuring the
safety of a new pipeline trans-shipping oil from the Negev
to the Mediterranean.

October 1956

Ben-Gurion participates in a secret conference with the
British and French at Sevres, France. He agrees to a combined
military operation whereby Israel will move to oust the
Egyptians from the trouble spots of Gaza and the Straits
of Tiran across the Sinai Peninsula. The British and French
will then intervene by parachuting into the Canal zone
ostensibly to make a buffer between Egypt and Israel.

29 October 1956

Israel invades Sinai and Gaza.

5 November 1956

Israel occupies the Tiran Straits and Gaza. The English have
second thoughts about seizing the Canal. A few French–
English paratroops drop into the zone. Then the USSR,
previously tied up by the Hungarian Revolution which it
has by this time successfully crushed, intervenes to
threaten Israel with invasion. The United States joins the
Russians in denouncing Israeli, French and British
intervention. The British and French pull out. Israel hangs on
trying to negotiate lasting guarantees regarding freedom of
navigation to Eilath and neutralization of Gaza which
remains a potential arrow pointed at its most developed
areas. UN troops occupy Gaza.

1 March 1957

Foreign Minister Mrs Golda Meir announces Israel's
withdrawal from the Sinai in return for guarantees through

the UN and endorsed by all the Great Powers that the Gulf of
Eilath is international water and must be open to all shipping.
The UN takes over the strategic points at the Straits of Tiran.

1957–60

Ben-Gurion, who at the time of the Suez war had re-assumed
the Prime Ministership, works to strengthen Israel's
international position by a series of alliances. The
rapprochement with France continues. An attempt is made to
have NATO guarantee Israel's frontiers but this comes
eventually to nought. A secret alliance is undertaken with
Ethiopia, Iran and Turkey all of which fear growing Arab
power in the Middle East, especially under Nasser.

March 1960

Ben-Gurion makes a tour of the major Western Powers.
The Eastern bloc is now inimical to Israel as Russia is heavily
backing the Arabs in its efforts to gain strength in the
Middle East. Ben-Gurion meets with President Dwight D.
Eisenhower in the United States and also with West
German Chancellor Konrad Adenauer who happens to be
there at the same time. He secures a five hundred million
dollar loan from Germany for development of the Negev.
Ben-Gurion also meets with British Prime Minister Harold
Macmillan in London and is warmly received by French
President Charles de Gaulle who extends the unprecedented
courtesy of inviting his visitor for a second meeting. Of
Ben-Gurion, General de Gaulle remarked on this occasion:
'I think that he and Adenauer are the two great leaders on
the Western side.' France is now Israel's closest ally.
Towards Germany, with which Israel is also maintaining
close relations despite strong opposition within the country,

Ben Gurion takes the attitude that having committed such terrible crimes against the Jewish people it must help Israel to establish itself. This is the only way it can begin to make redress for the wrongs committed in its name, Ben-Gurion feels.

23 May 1960

Adolf Eichmann, a principal administrator of the Nazi 'Final Solution', is captured by the Israeli Secret Service in Argentina. He is taken to Israel to stand trial and is executed on 31 May 1962.

Autumn 1960

Ben-Gurion is thinking of retirement to Sde Boker. Since 1957 he has gained, quite literally, a new lease of life by following the methods of Dr Moshe Feldenkreis. He lives a spartan life that includes Yoga exercises and a daily four-mile walk. Although more than seventy, Ben-Gurion has the vigour of a man of fifty-five. Nevertheless, he is tired of politics and is thinking of returning to the kibbutz.

An event then occurs that delays his retirement and causes him to leave office in the aftermath of a bitter dispute estranging him from many lifelong friends.

The event is a resurgence of the Lavon Affair. At this time, the Israelis catch the double agent who betrayed the Secret Service plot to the Egyptians. He indicates that Lavon may be innocent of complicity in the matter of ordering the operation to take place and that in any event there had been false testimony against him. Lavon immediately demands official rehabilitation. He comes to Ben-Gurion with whom he was once friendly. Ben-Gurion insists that the only correct way to resolve the whole affair is to call for a public judicial inquiry. Lavon furiously refuses to do this and publicly castigates Ben-Gurion and the Army for victimizing him in order, he says, to hide corruption within the military establishment.

The government other than Ben-Gurion want only one thing: to head off scandal. Over-ruling the Prime Minister, they vote to constitute a new Commission of seven members which will examine the Lavon case in secret hearing. This Commission hastily rehabilitates the former Defence Minister and drops the matter forthwith. Ben-Gurion is deeply disappointed that full judicial proceedings were not invoked to shed a wholly impartial light on the matter regardless of what lay behind it.

The Lavon Affair opens a rift in MAPAI between Ben-Gurion, allied with upcoming members of the young, indigenous Israeli generation, and the Prime Minister's old party associates of the generation immediately after his, the generation of the Third Aliyah. The latter resents what they term Ben-Gurion's autocratic ways. The former bitterly objects to the scurrying and face-saving methods utilized in dealing with Lavon.

December 1960

Israel and France build a nuclear reactor in the Negev. The Americans demand to know whether the reactor is to be used for military purposes and call for international control or immediate enforced inspection by American scientists. Ben-Gurion, always jealous of Israel's sovereignty, refuses inspection rights. The affair drags on through January 1961 when the Americans drop the matter.

July 1961

Israel launches its first rocket-missile.

Autumn 1961

Ben-Gurion is re-elected as Prime Minister. He faces a
restive Cabinet and Parliament.

1961–3

Ben-Gurion works to protect Israel against eventual
aggression by the Arab Federation. In an ultimate effort,
he tries to have both the USSR and the United States
guarantee Israel's frontiers. To no avail. Even the French will
conclude no formal, written alliance with Israel. De Gaulle
states grandly that relations between the two countries
are such that no formal alliance is necessary. Four years later,
he will make an about-face.

April 1963

President Itzhak Ben-Zvi dies. Ben-Gurion loses his last
surviving friend and most staunch supporter.

May 1963

Zalman Shazar becomes Israel's third President.

16 June 1963

Ben-Gurion abruptly resigns, returns to kibbutz Sde Boker
where he has lived ever since. Levi Eshkol succeeds him as
Prime Minister.

May 1964

The Lavon Affair crops up again when some MAPAI
leaders agitate for his return to government. Prime Minister
Eshkol goes so far as to write Lavon a letter declaring his
dismissal from government invalid. This rouses Ben-Gurion
who agitates for judicial proceedings.

Winter 1964

Ben-Gurion, who has made his own inquiry into the Affair,
submits a dossier to the Ministry of Justice saying that it
provides ample new evidence to warrant formal inquiry.
The Minister of Justice refuses to institute proceedings on the
grounds this could only be injurious to all concerned.

June 1965

Ben-Gurion stands for the Knesset (Parliament) at the head
of an Independent list made up mainly of younger men of
the generation of General Moshe Dayan. These have followed
Ben-Gurion out of MAPAI, and have formed the new RAFI
Party. He returns to the Knesset heading a list of ten delegates.
These delegates serve in coalition governments but Ben-
Gurion guides from afar at Sde Boker where he occupies
himself with:

i) Creating the College of the Negev which he hopes will
one day become a combination 'of Oxford University and
the Massachusetts Institute of Technology', and which
constitutes a permanent study centre both for the Negev and
on subjects directly related to the Negev's development.

ii) Writing the history of Israel's evolution as a state from
the First Aliyah in 1870 and 80 to his own departure from
government in 1963.

June 1967

The Arab nations once again demonstrate belligerency towards Israel. The Egyptians mass armour at Gaza and talk of invasion. They force the UN to abandon the strongholds of the Gulf of Eilath and again threaten Israeli shipping. The Syrians rain artillery fire from fortresses on the Golan Heights onto the Israeli kibbutzim in the valley below. Israel must retaliate or face a fight to the death on its own narrow territory.

5 June 1967

Egyptian forces bomb Israeli villages and cut off Eilath. Troops from Iraq, Algeria, Kuwait enter Egypt and make for Gaza. Troops from Saudi Arabia and Iraq join with the Army of Jordan on the Israel frontier. Troops in Syria mass at the Golan Heights.

6 June 1967–10 June 1967

Israel goes to war. The Israeli Army sweeps across the Sinai Peninsula, clears the Straits of Tiran and opens them once more to international shipping, takes over the near shore of the Suez Canal, occupies the massive underground Syrian fortresses of the Golan Heights, occupies the entire West Bank of the Jordan river. Operations last six days. On 7 June 1967 the capital of Jerusalem is joined in its totality to the nation. The ancient city, founded as the Jewish capital by King David in 1000 B.C.E. is whole again for the first time since Independence and its Jewish citizens can once more visit their age-old shrines in the eastern sector. Not since the Roman overthrow of the Jews in 70 C.E. has the city been totally in Jewish hands.

Mindful of the principle laid down by the United Nations and systematically violated under Jordanian rule that Jerusalem must be a place of worship for all, one of the Israeli government's first official acts is to guarantee protection and freedom of access to and worship at all shrines in the city, whether Jewish, Christian or Moslem.

29 January 1968

Paula Ben-Gurion dies.

2 May 1968

Israel celebrates its twentieth anniversary of nationhood.

Spring 1969

Ben-Gurion tours South Africa, South America and Europe calling for Jewish immigration to Israel and especially for young volunteers to work as pioneers in cultivating the desert.

BIBLIOGRAPHY

To complete his knowledge of the material which David Ben-Gurion evoked in the interviews on which this book is based, the editor referred to the following texts:

ARAD, Miriam. Review of David Ben-Gurion's *Letters To Paula* as published in Hebrew with the title *Michtavim El Paula*, Am Oved Publishers, Tel Aviv, 1968. Review in *Jerusalem Post*, 12 July 1968.

BAR-ZOHAR, Michael. *The Armed Prophet: A Biography of Ben-Gurion*. Translated from the French by Len Ortzen, Arthur Barker Limited, London, 1967.

BEN-GURION, David. *Israel: Years of Challenge*, Anthony Blond, London, 1964.

BEN-GURION, David. *Letters To Paula* as excerpted and translated into English by Mark Segal, *Jerusalem Post*, 28 February 1968.

BEN-GURION, David (ed.). *The Jews In Their Land*, Aldus Books, London, 1966.

The Holy Bible: King James Version.

CERCLE BERNARD LAZARE, Paris, June, 1968: *Conditions et Perspectives de Paix au Moyen Orient*. Articles by Herbert MARCUSE *et. al.*

DEROGY, Jacques. *Exode d'Europe 5707, Les Deux Exodes*, Denoël, Paris, 1968.

EPSTEIN, Rabbi Dr Isidore. *Judaism*, Penguin, Harmondsworth, 1959.

Facts about Israel 1969, Ministry of Information, Jerusalem, Israel.

GIVET, Jacques. *La Gauche Contre Israel*, J-J Pauvert, Paris, 1968.

LANDMANN, Salcia. *Der Jüdische Witz*, Walter-Verlag AG Olton, 1960, West Germany.

LITVINOFF, Barnet. *The Story of David Ben-Gurion*, Vallentine Mitchell, London, 1960.

LITVINOFF, Barnet. *A Peculiar People*, Weidenfeld and Nicolson, London, 1969.

PARKES, The Reverend James. *Arabs and Jews in the Middle East: A Tragedy of Errors*, Gollancz, London, 1967.

PARKES, The Reverend James. *A History of the Jewish People*, Penguin, Harmondsworth, 1962.

PEARLMAN, Lt.-Col. Moshe. *Ben-Gurion Looks Back*, Weidenfeld and Nicolson, London, 1965.

RAMATI, Segen-Aluf (Lt.-Col.) Shaul. *The Israel Defence Forces*, Handbook No. 4 in the series *Israel Today*, Jerusalem, 1966.

SAAB, Edouard. *L'Autre Exode, Les Deux Exodes*, Denoël, Paris, 1968.

SALOMON, Michel. *Israel: Le Royaume et l' Utopie*, Casterman, Brussels, 1968.

ZOHAR, Moshe. *Ben-Gurion as Military Strategist*. Article in the Newark, N.J., *Jewish News*, 1 February 1968.

ACKNOWLEDGEMENTS

Photographs by kind permission of Associated Press, London; Israel Embassy, London; Central Zionist Archives, Jerusalem; Israel Government Press Office, Jerusalem; Labour Archives, Tel-Aviv.